Rina
The Amazing story
of Recovery

D1557375

Survival

ISBN: 9798479869228

And:

Kerikeri
2021

Dedication

For Rina and our Whanau

Renene and Grahame Jelley

Pey Geldenhuys

Courtney and Lewis Chellew

Preston Gray Chellew

Brendan Jelley

Matthew, Lucy, Mia, and the late Jake Geldenhuys

And ALL our prayer warriors.

Contents

Rina's story

Introduction

This remarkable story is about the journey, from unexpected hospitalisation and through palliative care to the recovery, of my beautiful wife, Rina.

Palliative Care

Following complications of her admission to hospital and subsequent surgery, she was counselled by her Waikato hospital specialist doctors that there was little benefit in exposing her to the risks of further surgical intervention. They advised she, and her family, would need to decide whether stopping intervention and accepting care at home under palliative care was a decision she was comfortable with. She chose to accept a palliative care journey and to spend those days she had left, at her daughter's home, Wobble-Inn, if she was to die.

We were blown away by the number of well-wishes and "get well" messages and friends worldwide – with thanks to Facebook and other social-media contraptions like smart phones, tablets and modern communication "apps" like 'Messenger, Messages, WhatsApp, and Signal. Many folks shy away from the haze of applications available and tendency to 'just go Google -- -- or the internet'.

Transition to recovery

A special word of thanks is due to ALL the carers who have had a hand in Rina's miraculous recovery – with no less praise on our son-in-law Dr Grahame Jelley and my daughter Nurse Renene. At my last count Rina and I were humbled by receiving over 500 likes and 300+ Facebook comments and prayers. This is her story.

Prop Geldenhuys
Wobble-Inn
Kerikeri
17 September 2021

Survival

Whakapapa - Our past

Early courtship days – Kombisa Farm, Chatsworth, Rhodesia

Wedding of Prop and Rina

Breast Cancer and then a Stroke

Rina's first words, following her early stroke in 1993, following about six weeks of communicating with sign language, was the song "You are my sunshine" – sung while returning to Estcourt from a medical appointment in Pietermaritzburg.

you are my
SUNSHINE
my only sunshine
you make me
HAPPY
when skies are gray
you'll never know
dear how much
I LOVE YOU
please don't take
my sunshine away

Rina's story

"You are my Sunshine" speaks to me!

Our song that reminds us of the FIRST words spoken by Rina after her stroke some 30 years ago.

We were returing from an appoinment in Pietermaritzburg – While passing Mooi River, about 30 kms from home, the song came on the radio and I started singing and realised Rina was too! She spoke (or rather sang) about six weeks of being speechless. I was SPEECHLESS! So much so, I was forced to pull over because of the buckets of water (tears) falling from my eyes.

Survival

I just had to phone our kids as soon as I got home in Estcourt, Natal. And then got Rina to sing in the handset.

Rina's Colouring-In

Owl

Rina suffered a disabling stroke following her breast removal and cancer treatment plus stroke about thirty years ago (1993). She was paralysed on her right-hand side, blind in one eye, partial hearing in her right ear and left with a significant speech impediment of high

Rina's story

frequency sounds, that left her with very little ability to express herself. She retained her ability to understand and often is frustrated with her inability to speak out her thoughts in a meaningful way. As an outlet for her expression, she took up crochet work of a home-made frame and then progressed to colouring in books – while my hobby was converting manuscripts into e-books. These are but a few of her pictures.

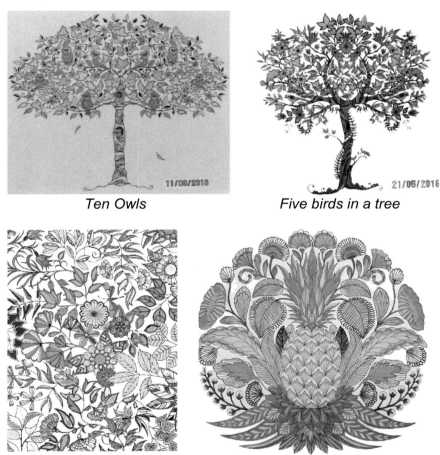

Ten Owls　　　　　　*Five birds in a tree*

Rina's　　　　　*Sketch by THS friend on Facebook*

Survival

2016 Drawings

2017 Book by Paul and Karen

Brother Phil Malan's Sketches

Phil is not a Facebook man – unlike me! We had lost contact after he tried to emigrate to Scotland some seven years ago. Once Rina was moved to 'palliative care' my son managed to re-establish comms with Phil and Elcora Malan. He soon surprised us with posting his superb drawings on 'Rina's Hospitalisation site on WhatsApp.

See back of the book for more wildlife, animals, actors, cars and now trains.

My wife, Rina is on my mind! Day 60 of Palliative Care? You Go, Girl!

The above Facebook posting was made on Day 60 (23 July 2021) and day 100 is my planned book launch for all those people wanting 'pre-launch special offers!

Prayer warriors for Rina

Herewith my list of prayer warriors. They are listed alphabetically, by surname (and the Index, alphabetically by Christian names). Only some Facebook comments + emojis, are shown (go to back of book):

Grant Alborough: - My thoughts and prayers are with you both. God bless. Peter Allan. Stewart Allen: - A lot of us thinking of you Prop. Sure, my friend. Geoff Antlett: - Wish you both all the best through these difficult times. Prop, yes with pleasure + a smily face emoji. Mark Aitchison; Richard Aslin: - Thoughts are with you. Retha Baker. Cyndi Barker: - Wishing her Godspeed.
Our daughter Renene and son Pey arranged smartphone WhatsApp and Messenger postings. Courtney favoured Signal postings. Mostly reproduced herewith (some with permission, others not [Too much of a hassle, SOB])

See back of the book, just before the Index, for the prayer warriors for Rina (Continued..)

Hospital Stay

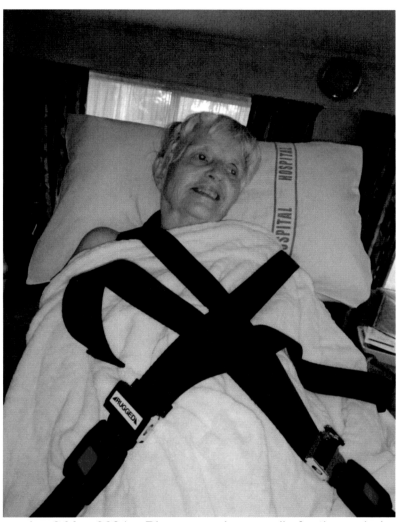

Thursday 6 May 2021 – Rina managing a smile for the ambulance transfer to Hospital – the last time she would be in her home in Paeroa. She had suffered on and off the previous days in pain and difficulty keeping anything down.

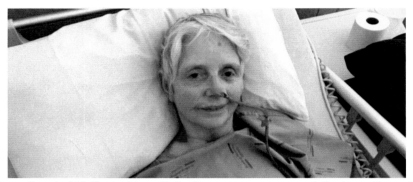

Transfer to Waikato Hospital after an assessment that confirmed a bowel obstruction.

A nasogastric tube inserted to decompress the stomach and bowel. The first conservative measures were to see if this would allow the bowel to resolve – Grahame likened this to an escalator not allowing food to move beyond the obstruction. Unless there is a twist or physical obstruction, the bowel sometimes can function again but in moms' case this was the case as the bowel was caught up in a herniation.

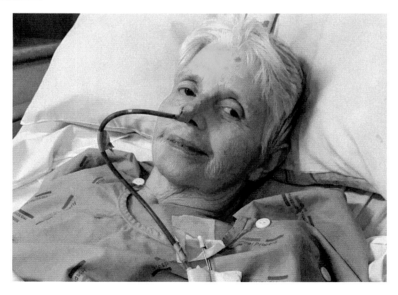

Rina's story

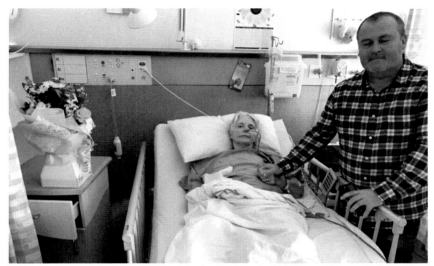

Pey and dad followed the ambulance to Waikato Hospital on the Thursday and mom was kept nil per mouth. They brought Rina's Mother's Day flowers from Grahame & Renene sent from Kerikeri.

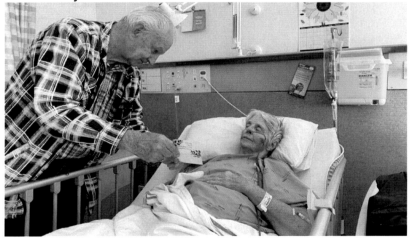

Reading a card from Grahame & Renene for Mother's Day

Mother's Day flowers to add some cheer

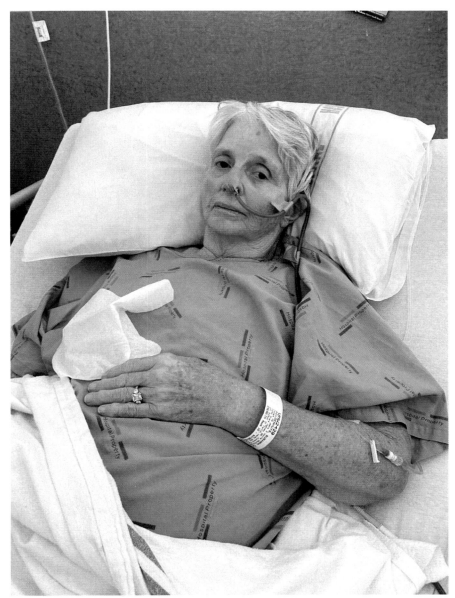

Friday 7 May – "Drip and Suck" the term used to rest the bowel with the Nasogastric tube and only feed with intravenous fluids

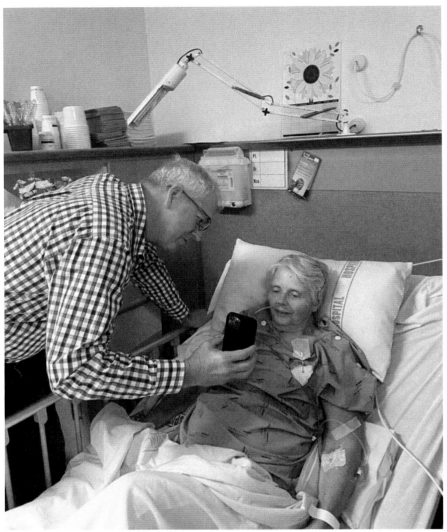

Saturday 8 May – Grahame & Renene drove through the night before from Kerikeri. Rina's status not improving and a CT and Xray confirms the obstruction and bowel also perforated and possibly will need a colostomy/stoma. We waited anxiously to hear from the doctors over the weekend when surgery will happen - Grahame showing pictures explaining what is happening prior to surgery.

Rina's story

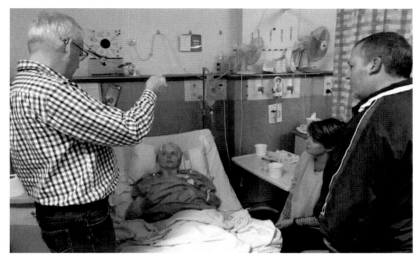

*Renene managed to give Rina the last shower and hair wash she
would have for a while as she managed to get up into a wheelchair
on the Sunday– appropriately done on Mother's Day.*

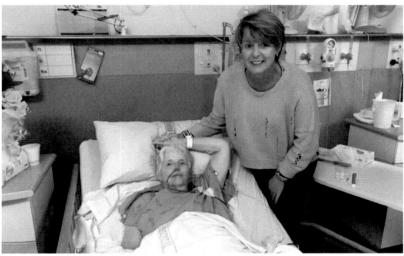

*Brave faces anticipating going into theatre soon! The staff allowed
us to follow Rina and remain with her in the Pre-op room before
wheeling her into the theatre. The porter was from Pietermaritzburg
and reassured Rina speaking in Afrikaans "totsiens".*

ICU to HCU – High Care Unit

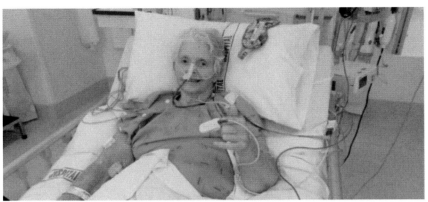

Rina in HCU, *managed a brave 'thumbs up' sign*
9 May – Sunday and Mother's Day. 8 hours later after emergency
surgery. A relief that Rina pulled through the surgery and
anaesthetic and did not have a colostomy – they had resected the
bowel and she was responding well post op.

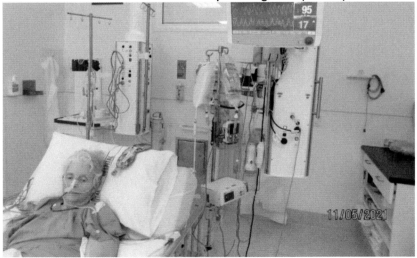

Rina moved from "ICU to HCU and then to M12" in Waikato
Hospital. Then to Ward Room 6. She was allowed only limited
visitors.

Rina's story

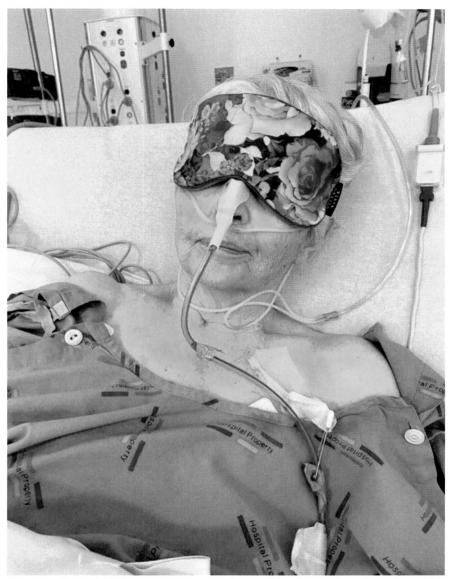

Renene bought Rina an eye covering to block out the glare from the bright hospital fluorescent lights.

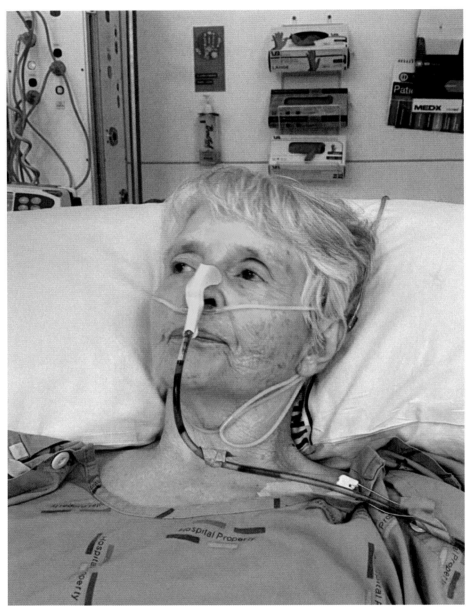

Getting tired of the elephant trunk and oxygen tubing

High Care Unit visit

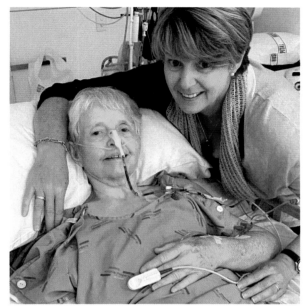

A smile post op – in the High Care Unit with Renene

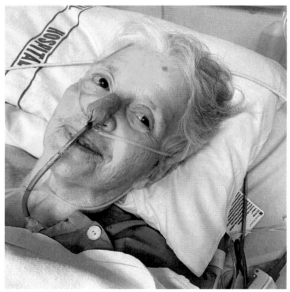

High on drugs in the High Care Unit

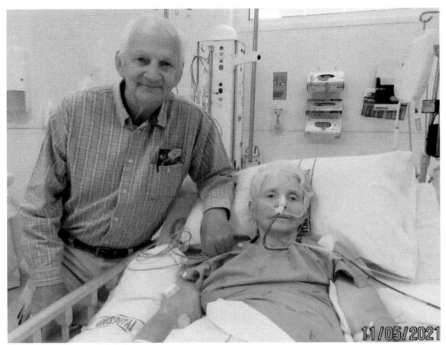

Rina about to farewell 'HCU'" for single bed Room 6 in Ward M12

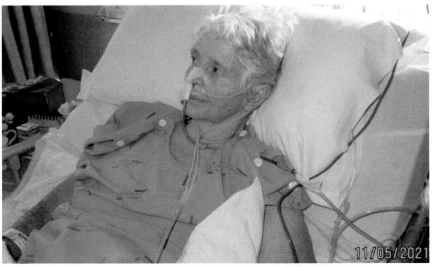

A private room made a huge difference

Camping in Hamilton

Camping in Hamilton

Fast asleep

Wide awake

Pey and Prop camping at the Hamilton Tourist Park near the hospital.

Rina's story

Renene 'Glamping" in a little Air B & B which looked onto Rina's hospital ward. She could walk back and forth safely late at night after sitting with Rina.

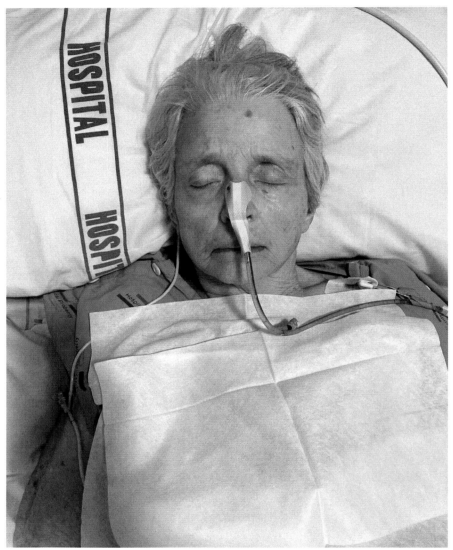

Rina struggling with not being able to sleep with all the noises and interruptions in the ward. She was transferred from the High Care Unit to M12 (surgical) – the staff kindly gave her a private room. We were so grateful, but this still did not provide Rina much rest post operatively.

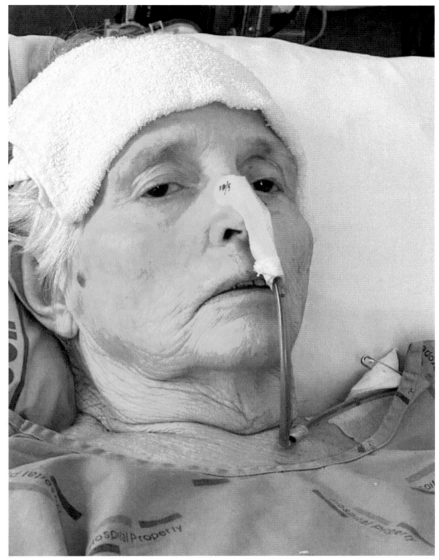

A cool face cloth to help with the fevers and nausea – Rina starting to decline again after the surgery.

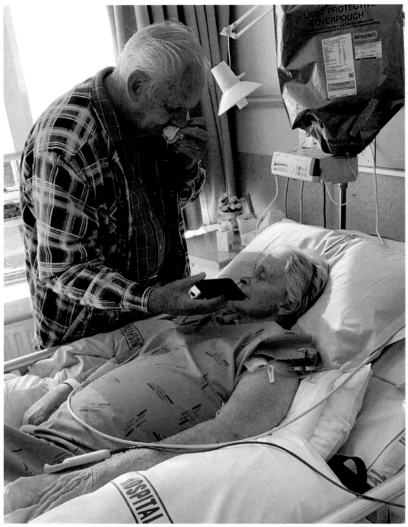

Sharing messages with Rina as each day she starts to deteriorate as unable to keep anything down. Her nutrition bag dripping sustenance as her body goes into the second week of very little nutrition and her protein levels drop dangerously low. Her abdomen started to retain extra cellular fluid and organs started to not cope with the fluid balance.

Rina's story

Prayers and encouragement when feeling awful and despondent as the bowel appears to not be coping with the resection and the abdominal wound splits open requiring plugging and dressings- it too becomes infected. With a poor nutritional status, there is not much healing.

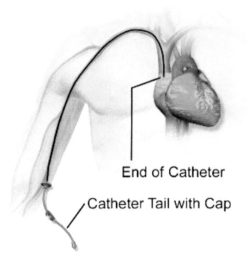

End of Catheter

Catheter Tail with Cap

A PICC Line had to be inserted into Rina's vein in her arm to administer long term intravenous antibiotics, nutrition and medications and allow them to draw blood daily to check how Rina was responding. The PICC line however failed twice as her veins were not coping – they started to administer TPN (Trans parenteral nutrition) via the nasogastric tube on an hourly basis.

A framed card from the church community in Paeroa. We would read messages from family and friends from SA, Zim and NZ - a very emotional time watching the reactions of Prop and Rina of all the love and heartfelt prayers for her recovery and comfort.

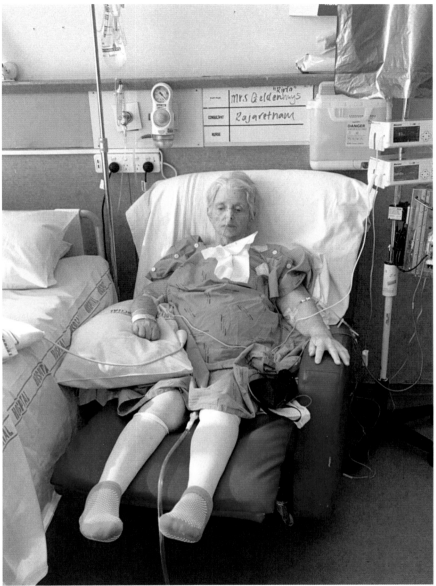

Despite feeling poorly Rina has daily physiotherapy and gets up at least once a day. Not an easy process with all the tubing from top to bottom!

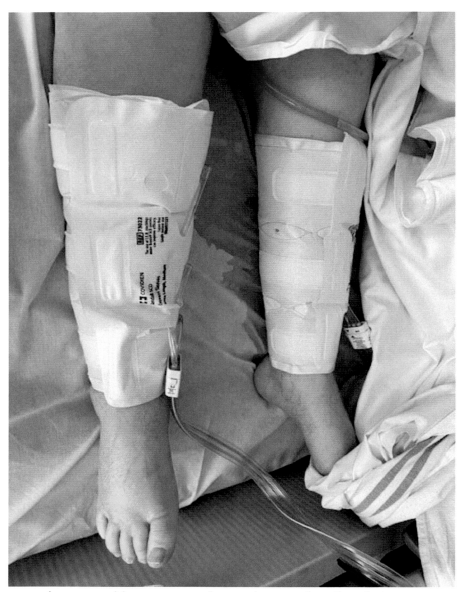

Legs requiring compression and support as they become oedematous and weep excess fluid accumulation. The organs not coping removing toxins.

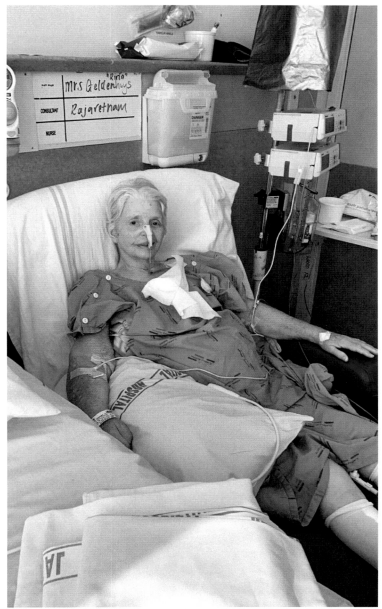

Resting up after getting short of breath on exertion – fluid now on the lungs.

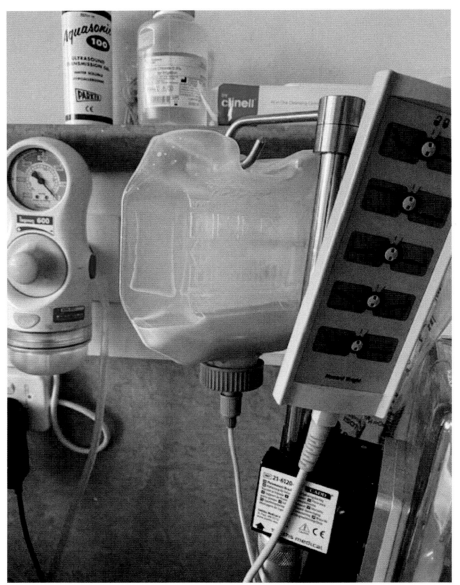

Protein supplement, "Ensure" given via the nasogastric tube throughout the night in an attempt to give some nutrition.

Rina's story

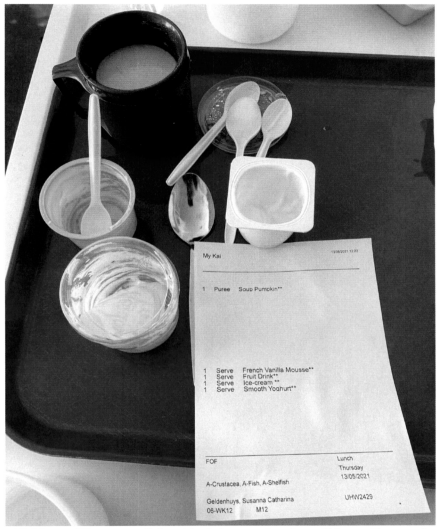

13 May – Rina on soft food but does not eat anything – Prop eats what is on the tray for her. Rina would only mange a teaspoon of ice cream and maybe 50 ml soup.

Survival

Waikato Hospital cafeteria – dinner on the run in between sitting next to Rina. Looking for the silver lining.

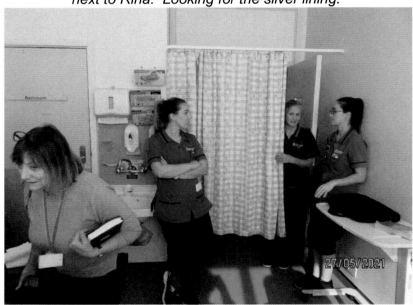

Novelle Farrell, Savanna , Ann and Alex – all-stars with Rina about to be go to Wobble-Inn

Visitors in Hospital

On Monday 17th May, Pastor Cliff and Patricia Kershaw from Elim Paeroa visited and prayed for Rina.

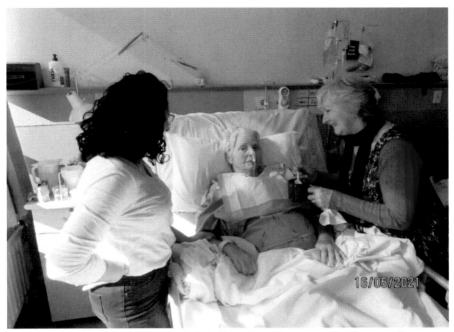

Dee McColl and Chanli Brink feeding Rina – with Cuppa Soup

Phil and Carolyn Runciman gave Rina a surprise visit plus Carolyn read Rina a story. They left to look for Ivan Myocevich , a fellow Elim Church member also sick but returned later without finding him. He sadly died at 9:30 pm that night.

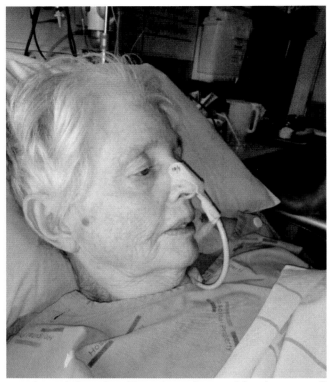

Rina enjoyed Carolyn Runciman's weekly story readings.

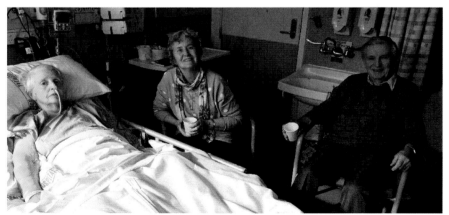

Phil and Carolyn Runciman visited Rina. Carolyn did weekly storybook reading for Rina at Beulah.

Rina's story

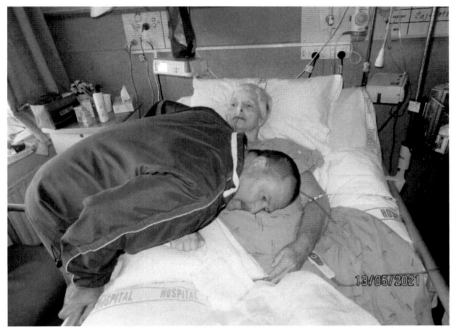

Pey listening for stomach noises

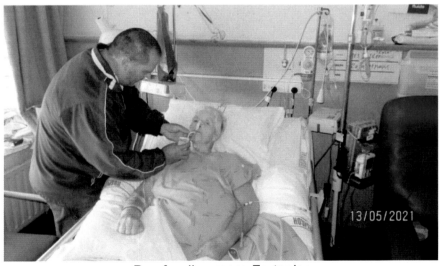

Pey feeding mom Fortasips

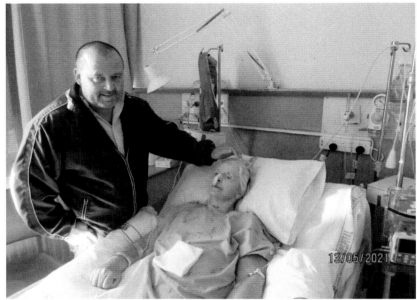

Pey staying in Hamilton with Rina and Prop returns to Paeroa and he travels back and forth every second day.

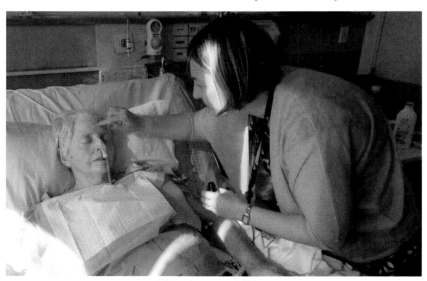

Heather and Rina

Rina's story

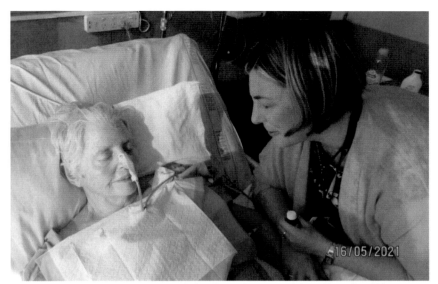

16/05/2021 Heather visited and prayed healing for Rina

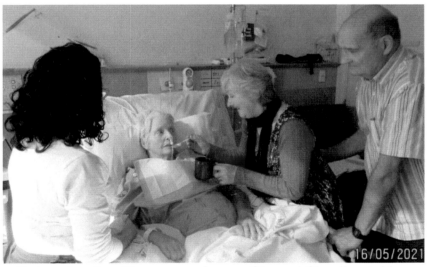

Delene feeding Rina a cup of soup. Stu and Chanli watching.

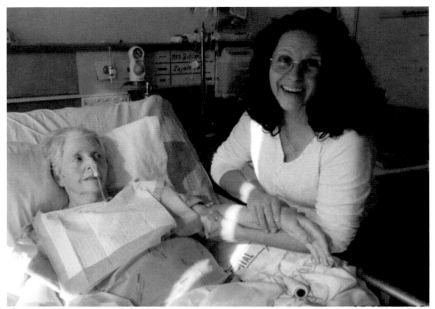

Wonder-woman Chanli Brink always has a smile

Flowers for a very special person
The next day, Tyrone and Wendy Chisnall and Pamela Aranos
phoned Rina.

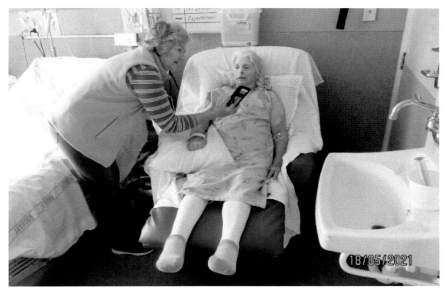

Delene showing Rina a video clip on hey smart phone. Note the white stockings on Rina's swollen feet.

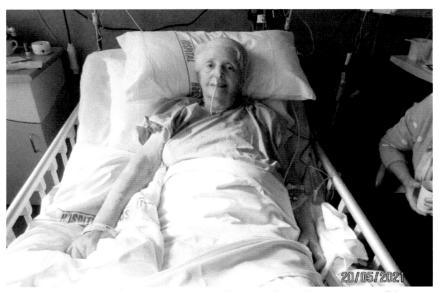

Visitor Carolyn Runciman – reading stories always gave Rina a smile

Rensh, Chanli and Charlie visit and attempt to get a smile from Rina

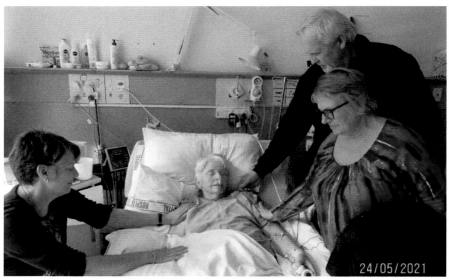

Ps Cliff and Patricia laid hands on and prayed for Rina

Rina's story

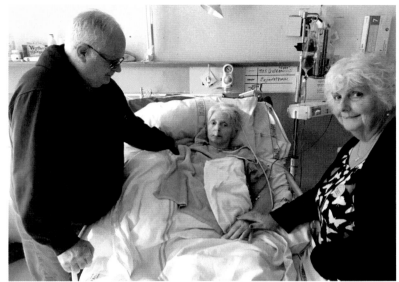

*Elim Super Seniors Ken and Dawn Kershaw visited and prayed for
Rin*

*Elim elder Ken Kershaw prayed a blessing on our anniversary date.
They (Ken and Dawn) visited us in Waikato. Ken and Dawn
Kershaw visited Rina in Hospital*

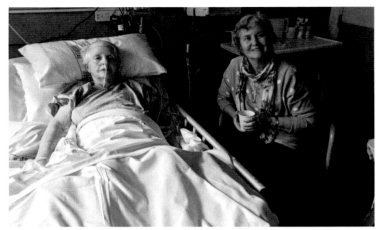

Carolyn Runciman always did story reading for Rina

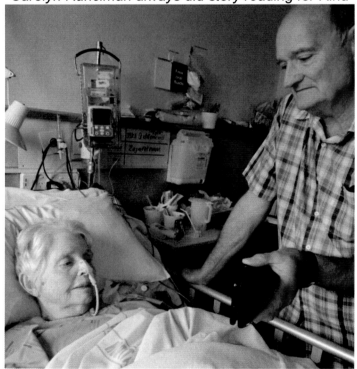

Stu McColl sharing messages on phone

Rina's story

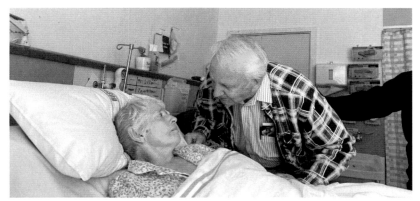

A tender moment realising that Rina was not doing well after the operation. Her family are with her every day for the last week in hospital as the doctors do more tests to determine what the complications are.

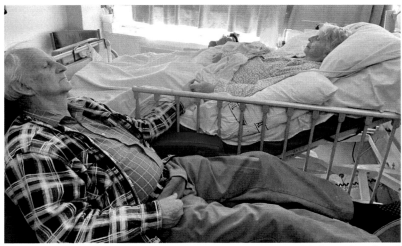

Exhausted with the news and emotional load of informing family near and far the bad news that the CT scan shows the bowel resection was compromised and the ascites was undermining her healing. Rina has a paracentesis done to relieve some of the abdominal fluid building up. The procedure drained nearly 2 litres of abdominal fluid and made Rina more comfortable. It also took off the strain of organs trying to cope.

Surrounded by her loved ones – the nasogastric tube is removed to provide Rina as much comfort as the decision to palliate has been made and make her as comfortable and pain free as possible.

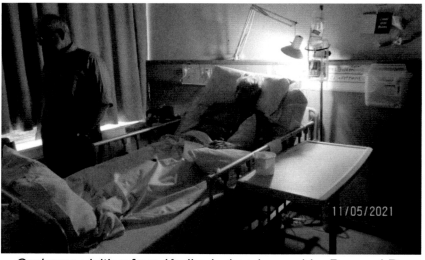

Grahame visiting from Kerikeri when he could – Pey and Renene would alternate weeks at the hospital in Hamiltong except for the last week when the family were all together with Rina with the big decisions made about her management.

Rina's story

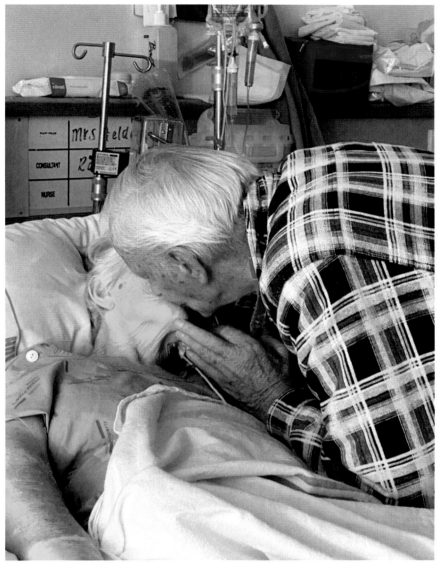

Each good night kiss difficult as unsure if Rina will survive the night.

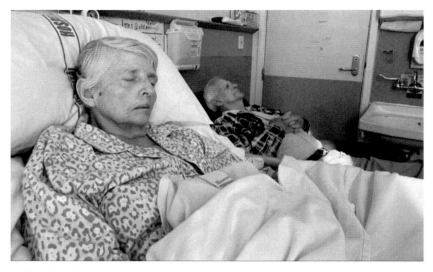

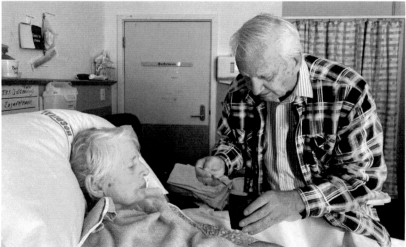

After some of the abdominal fluid was drained, Rina felt like some soup. This was very encouraging, but she had bouts of nausea and vomiting so we had to be careful how much she could tolerate. She started to lose weight daily.

Rina's Waikato Carers

There are just too many to name ALL of them now. However – to top the list includes our children for offering up so much for us – Renene Jelley and Pey Geldenhuys. Dr Grahame Jelley has moved mountains in making our stay at Wobble-Inn as comfortable as possible. Also, my sister Delene and her husband Stu McColl of Beulah in Paeroa.

I would also acknowledge, the nursing staff, doctors and backroom people of Waikato Hospital, Hamilton. Doctors Nigel Rajavetnam and Doctor Cameron, Nurses Anne, Aimee, Alex, Haley, Stacey, Savanna and several whose names escapes me, did their bit as well.

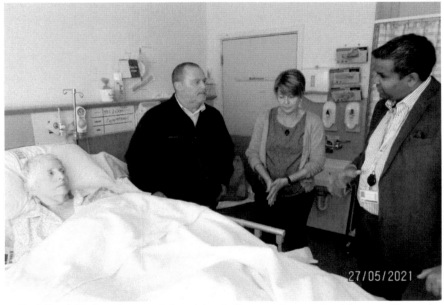

Dr Nigel Rajaretnam doing his daily ward rounds. He mentioned that Palliative care staff Dr Cameron and Nurse Novelle Farrell would make discharge arrangements for Rina.

So impressed with the Waikato nurses – but especially Charge Nurse Anne, and Nurse Alex .The Nurses were awesome

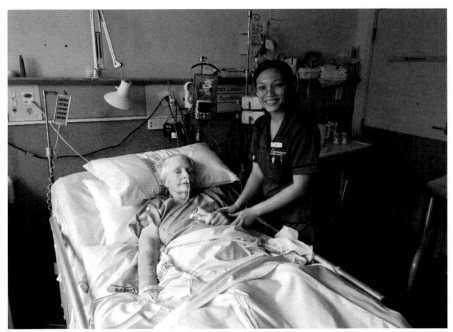

Nurse Joy-Ann Delrosario tending to Rina 20 May

Rina's story

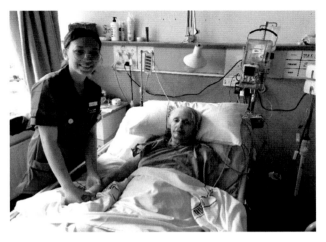

Nurse Joy from Harare, Zimbabwe

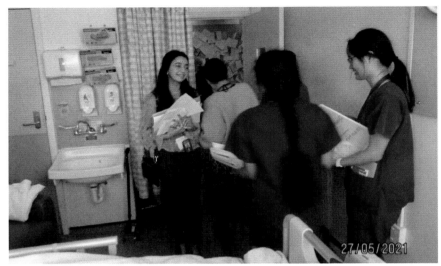

The doctors left before I could take my normal 'picture'.

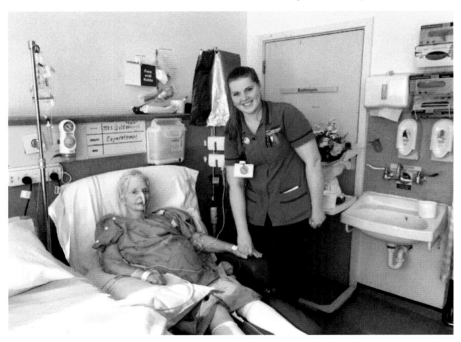

Physio assistance

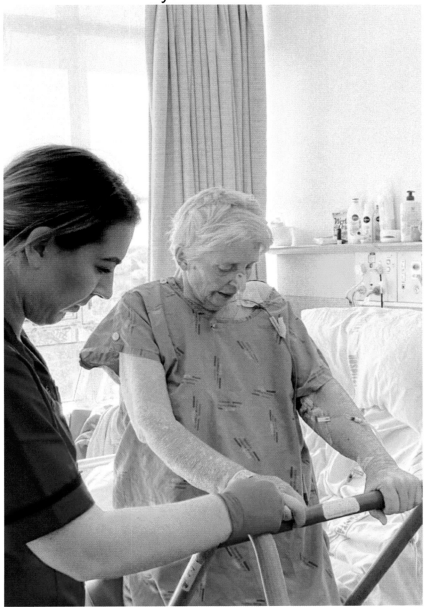

Nurse Savanna helping Rina with daily physiotherapy sessions

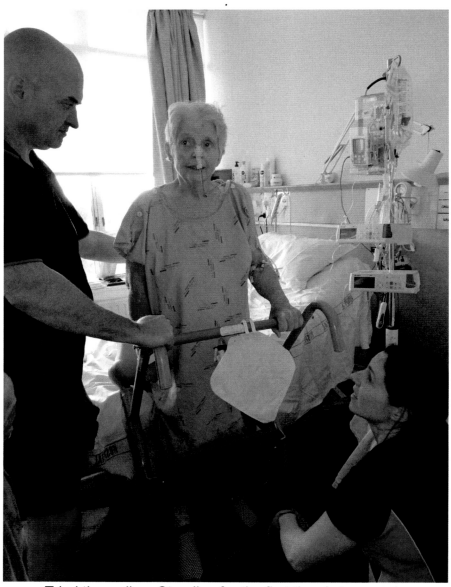

Tried the walker. Standing for the first time in two weeks

Rina's story

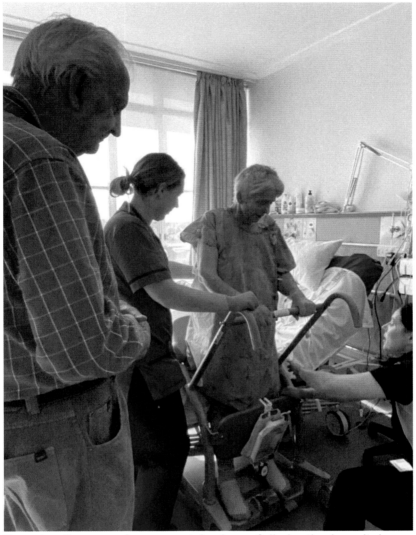

Rina standing on a frame, watched carefully by the hospital nurse and physiotherapist. This was perhaps the 'last time' that Rina managed to keep her balance – by herself – date: 18 May 2021. – the last time this feat was managed. Also Weighing Rina – she put on 11kg with fluid retention

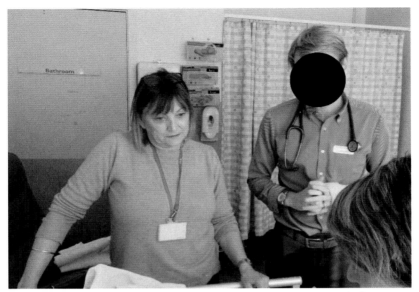

Palliative care staff, Novelle Farrell with Dr Cameron – discussing Rina's wishes to spend her remaining days at Wobble-Inn, Kerikeri.

Bevan And Aimee – photo taken the Saturday before my 'count down' commenced

Rina's story

Glenys – the ward health care assistant who was always cheerful

Health care assistant Glenys.

The Transfer - Friday 28 May 2021 to Wobble Inn

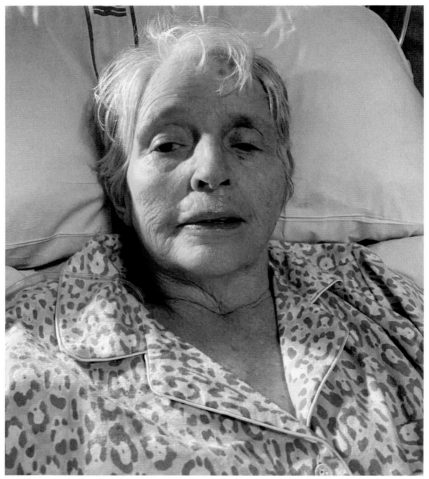

Rina without her nasogastric tube and her IV line. Acceptance that the next journey will be by ambulance to Kerikeri. A restful night sleep as now on a syringe driver administering pain medication that the Hospice team will manage once in Kerikeri. Honouring Rina's wishes to die at Wobble Inn with family. Thurs 27 May

Rina's story

Nurse Alex and Savanna handing over to Mike the Paramedic who will transfer Rina to Kerikeri. The cost of the transfer was $2500 for the 5-7 hour journey from Hamilton to Kerikeri – Wobble Inn.

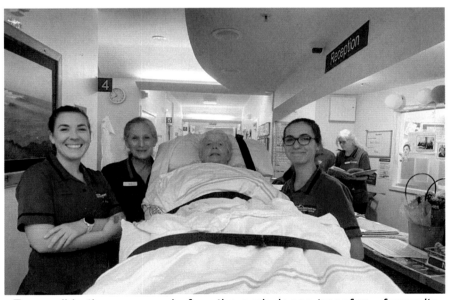

Farewell in the passage before the ambulance transfer – favourite nurses Savanna, Charge Nurse Anne and Alex. Heartfelt good byes and grateful for their kind care.

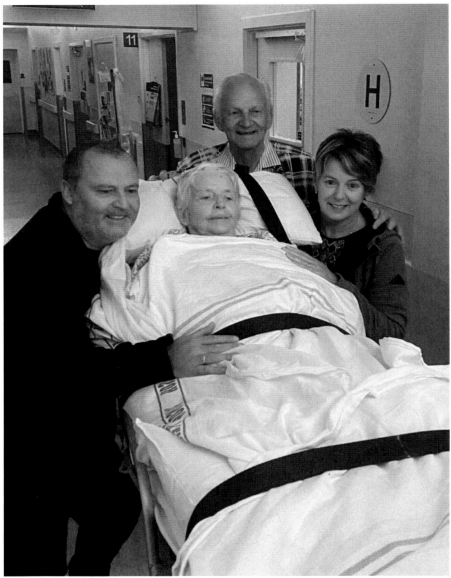

*Renene would remain with Rina in the ambulance trip and Pey and
Prop would follow after collecting things via Paeroa.*

Rina's story

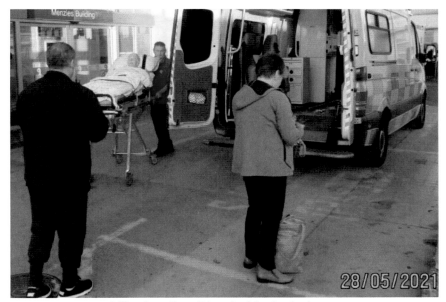
Mike loading Rina in his Ambulance

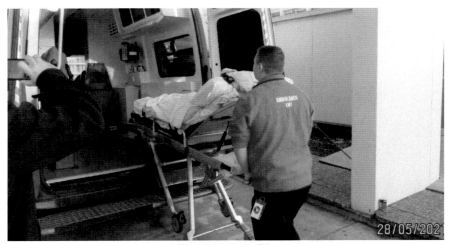
Mike loading Rina

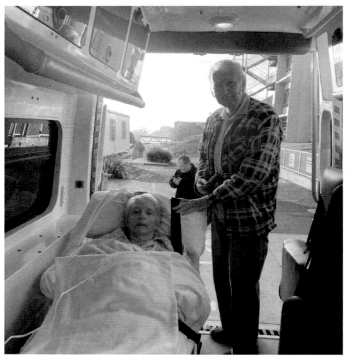

Ready for a long trip on bumpy roads.

Mercedes Benz private ambulance

Rina's story

Private ambulance transfer – Friday, 28 May 2021.

Rina recognising we are driving through Auckland and over the Harbour Bridge – another 3 hours travel to go. The Skytower is vizible through the window.

Kerikeri Carer team

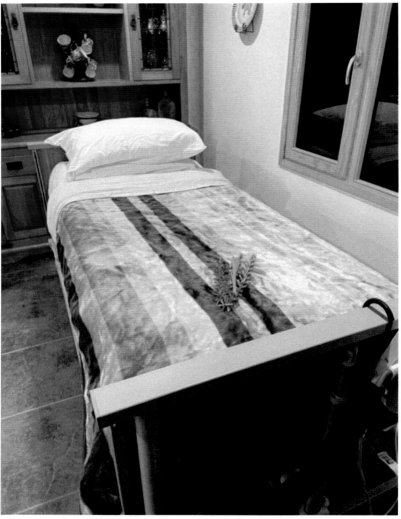

Grahame stuck at home arranged all the hospice equipment needed for Rina's comfort including the hospital bed all prepared for her arrival

Rina's story

Kelly Brown, Geneva Health Care worker has been most helpful, especially prepared to come tend to Rina during the Stage 4 Lockdown.

(Kelly Brown enjoys a fascinating whakapapa, which her Kaumatua can trace back for 26 generations. She did her schooling in Lower Hut and Wellington and currently lives at Okaihau- . She loves good motorcars and is very proud of her two daughters.)

Health Care worker Pam, is absolutely adored by Rina for her gentle manner, care, and bed baths'. She always chats away with Rina and leaves her smiling.

Both Rina and Pam give a thumbs-up to the job Pam enjoys doing.

1st June, day No 8. Claire Orchard –the nurse from Geneva Healthcare came in to do initial caregiver assessment when Rina after a Hospice referral to assist with care giving

Hospice Nurse adjusting Rina's medication.

Karen and Paul Geldenhuys visited Wobble-Inn on the 6th June 2021. He and Pey Geldenhuys built the deck for the Campervan. It was also Grahame & Renene anniversary and they could disappear for a couple of hours to have a dinner celebration in town.

29 May Thandi very perceptive that Rina not well.

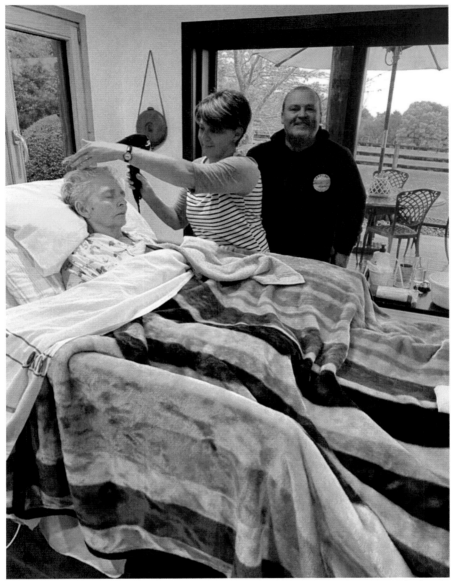

Saturday 29 May – the first of many hair salon appointments in bed.

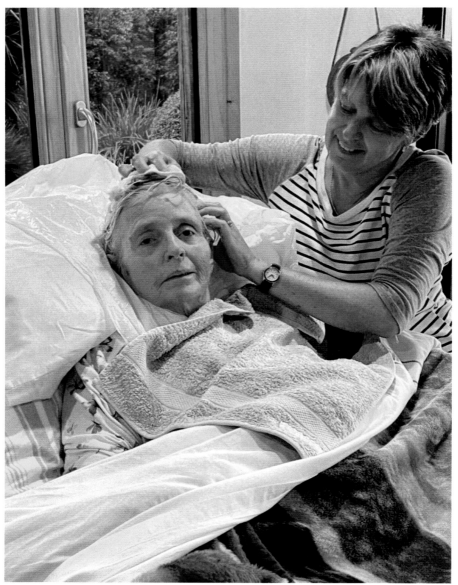

Using special microwave heated shampoo and conditioner caps that Hospice provided to give the scalp a good massage

Rina's story

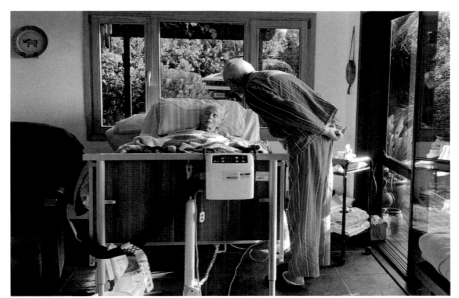

Every morning is a blessing. Prop staying in the spare room close by in the initial days.

28 May – the first night Rina came home to Kerikeri – Prop remained vigil for most of the night next to Rina.

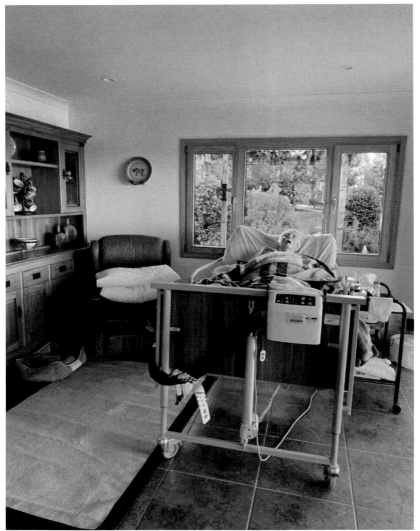

Rina mostly drugged on the Hospice medication – Grahame started to intervene and change the dose administration according to symptoms and Rina started to become more alert and started to tolerate more and more fluids. It would take a month before Rina would start to eat anything solid – soft baby food to start with. Bone broth and protein replacement "Ensure" became a daily intake.

Monday 31 May – the reason to have a room with a view is that when awake – Rina could enjoy the view and "wild-life" at Wobble Inn.

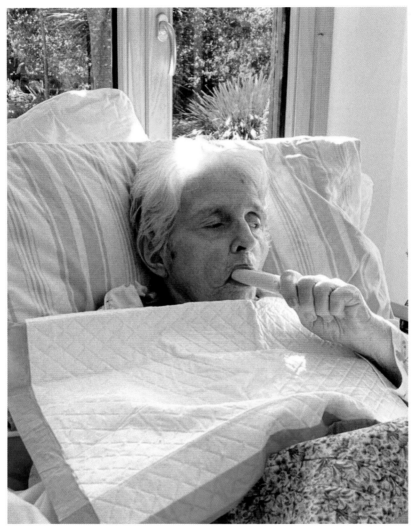

Tuesday 1 June – managing an ice block – tide starting to turn and Rina's colour improving as Grahame and Renene work hard to address her fluid balance and symptom management. The bowel starts to respond normally to a soft food diet and Rina's oesophagus starts to heal after the trauma from the long-term nasogastric tube presence. We elect to take her off the oxygen at night as she appears to be coping without it.

Rina's story

Tuesday 2 June - District Nurse Lorraine Mabidikama comes in for a wound and catheter check – She is also from Zimbabwe and her husband Ezra is a colleague of Grahame's. Ezra was the Doctor present when Rina arrived at Wobble-Inn with the ambulance transfer.

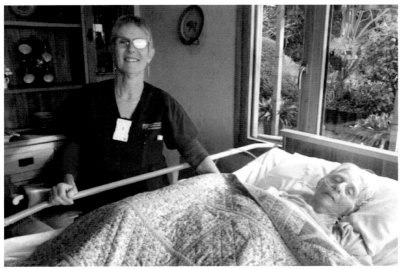

District Nurse Prue who has subsequently retired

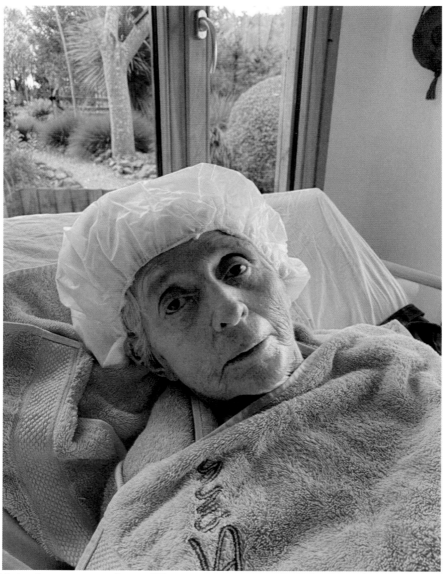

Hair shampoo and conditioner caps warmed up in the microwave can be very relaxing whilst they do their job!

Care giver Pam gives Rina the salon treatment

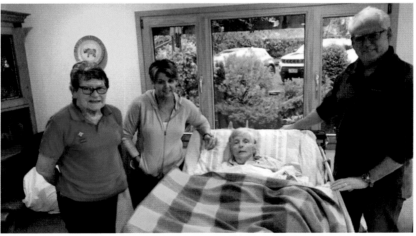

The "A" Team – Pam, nurse Rina and Dr. Grahame

Friday 4 June – Rina did not have such a good night as some fluid on the lungs. Grahame together with the hospice team change her medication again and started her on oxygen again. There is concern she will need another paracentesis to remove fluid from the abdomen. Nigel Payne, her new GP in Kerikeri visited her twice to assess if this was indicated but felt the risks were too high to introduce infection. We continued to treat Rina conservatively and kept her on just oral fluids.

"Thumbs up"

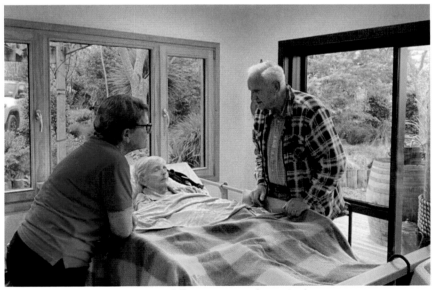

Pam and Prop swapping stories

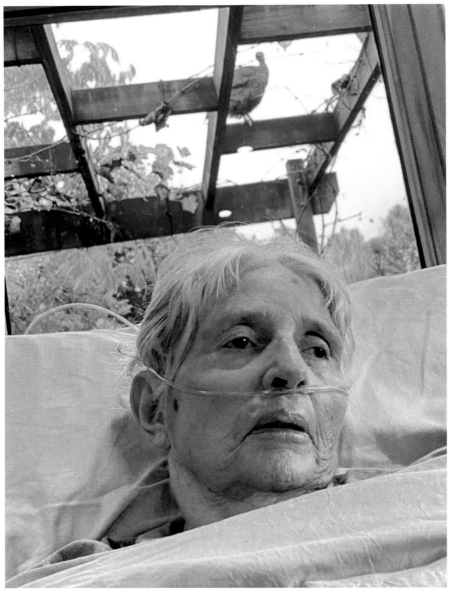

6 June - A guinea fowl sits watching Rina from the pergola. Oxygen is required day and night.

12 June – Pey travels through from Auckland on the weekend to see Rina – he notices the weight loss. Lounge lizards!

Thandi sensing there may be concerns with Rina's health

Sat 12 June – Smoking a peace pipe Attempting to expand Rina's lungs as much as possible with a party toy!

Rina's story

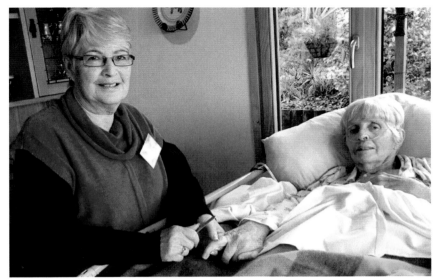

Hospice care giver Tiri comes in to sit with Rina, does the tricky right hand nail cutting, whilst Grahame and Renene travel to Whangarei for Grahame's treatment

Reading messages and prayers from family.

Tuesday 8 June – attempting to sit up on the Hospice air bed requires lots of support. Rina quite anxious having been bed bound now for months.

Totally exhausted from the "physio" session

Rina's story

Dr Grahame listening to Rina's lungs

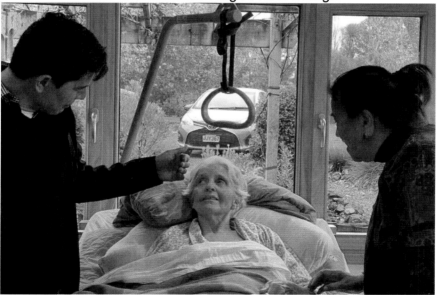

Samuel Cruickshank and his mother (a Pastor's wife) visiting Rina

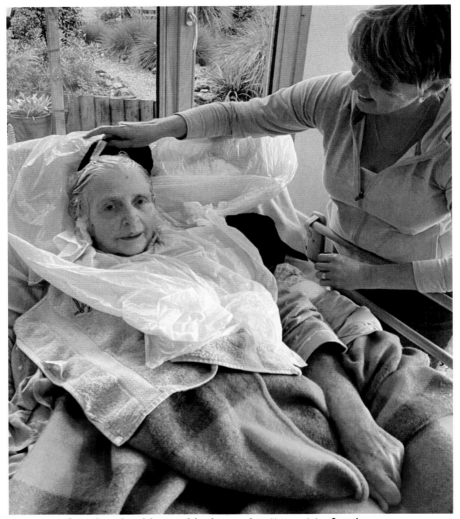

Another bed bound hair wash attempt to freshen up

Rina's story

Sunday 13 June – some progress and eating more and more soft food AND feeding herself. Mouth ulcers and we assume damage from the nasogastric tube had caused some trauma and made swallowing difficult. Grahame and Renene tried numerous treatments to sort out her oral care with success eventually. A good sign was Rina was getting quite fussy what she wanted and did not want to eat!

Survival

A game of charades – trying to understand what is being communicated can be very difficult and frustrating for all – especially Rina. "Dinges" that word she has never forgotten since her stroke is always in the vocabulary of Charades/guessing what she wants or has to say!

Palliative Care Nurses

Jo Bolter   Pip Field

Rina's story

Kaput! Sunday 13 June – Prop drove with Pey to Paeroa to pick up some belongings and fill his car with as much as possible and then drove back to Kerikeri all in the same day! He did not want to leave mom even for one night! A 6-hour journey one way on a good day driving through Auckland traffic.

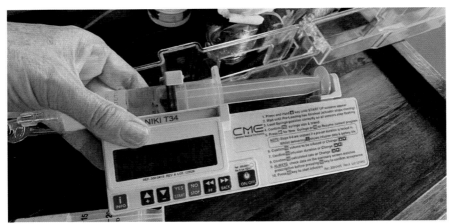

Syringe Driver that administered powerful medications to keep Rina comfortable

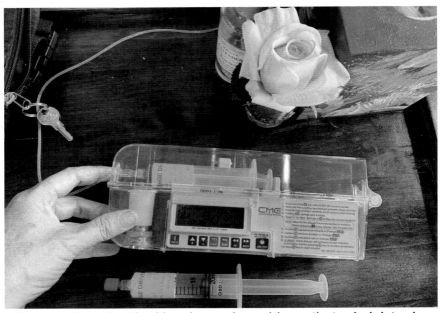

Renene changing the Hospice syringe drivers that administer her medications. Grahame worked with the Hospice team to start looking at a rehabilitative approach and wean her off all the narcotics and sedating medication. We started to see the old Rina return.

Guinea fowl antics

Saturday 12 June - Vitamin D therapy. The first time Rina has been outside in a very long time. Grahame, Pey and Prop manually moved Rina into the Lazy boy and wheeled her out onto the deck.

Wobble Inn on a winter's day

Thank goodness for technology. Prop on computer and Rina watching Christian movie channel.

Going through facebook memories and remembering bygone days

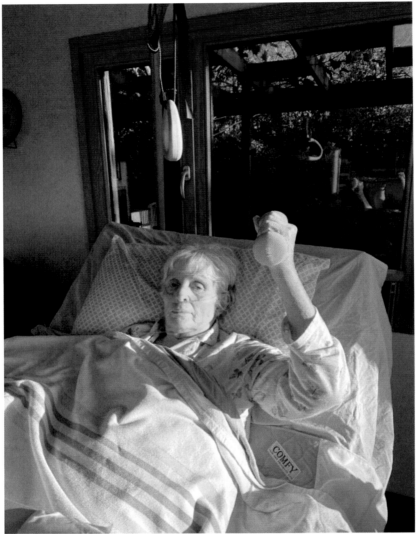

Wednesday 16th June Early arm exercises. Later in the day the Palliative Doctors (Dr Warwick Armstrong and Dr Anita Patel) visited and decision to taper down syringe driver medication significantly and take a more rehabilitative than palliative approach. Still dependent on oxygen as short of breath through the day and night.

The Wobble Inn "ward" – animals allowed to attend visiting hours. Monday 21st June.

21 June – watching Elim Church services. Note the earphones

Diversional therapy important in rehabilitation. Rina still struggling with swallow of fluid and using Preston's "sippy cup"

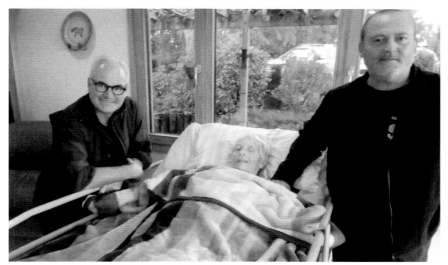

Dr Nigel Cane's second 'house visit, recommending transfer to Bay of Island hospital for blood transfusion.

Caravan bed made for Rina -complete with TV and Radio

Overnight transfusion in Bay of Islands Hospital, Kawakawa.

Wednesday 23rd June 2021

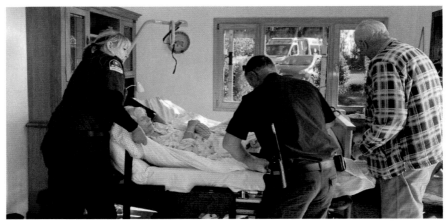

Ambulance crew uplifting Rina before transfer to ambulance to Bay of Island hospital.

Hard Yaka getting stretcher across the grass. At least was a sunny day and Rina got outdoors

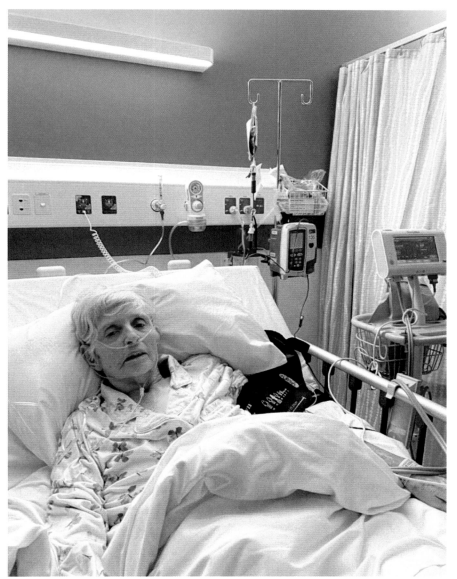

The hospital commenced two-unit blood transfusion throughout the night

Survival

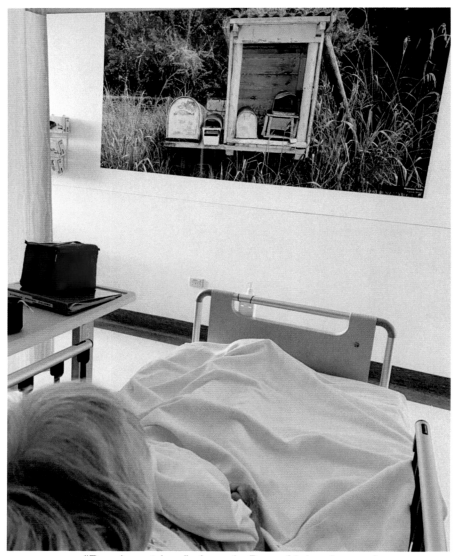

"Rural post-box" views in Bay of Islands ward

102

Ready to return home to Wobble Inn. Still only managing to drink broth.

Pey visiting from Auckland and supervising in the "gym" on 27th June 2021

More diversional therapy

Rina's story

Rina was encouraged to take up her colouring in – to exercise her only hand to "function" to grip her walking stick/reclaim her balance.

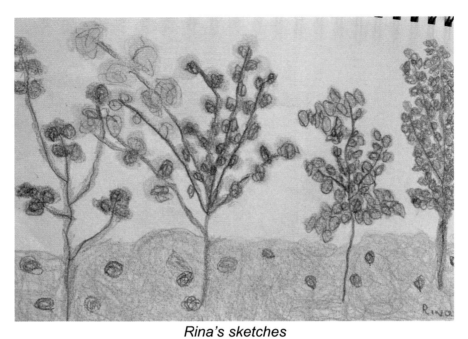

Rina's sketches

Two freehand pictures by Rina

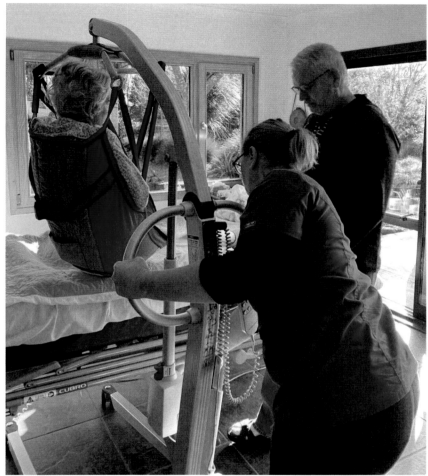

Mary Bowe, Occupational therapist showing us how to move Rina with a hoist. Beginning of liberation of Rina from being confined to bed constantly.

Hoist transfer – bed to chair and vice-versa.

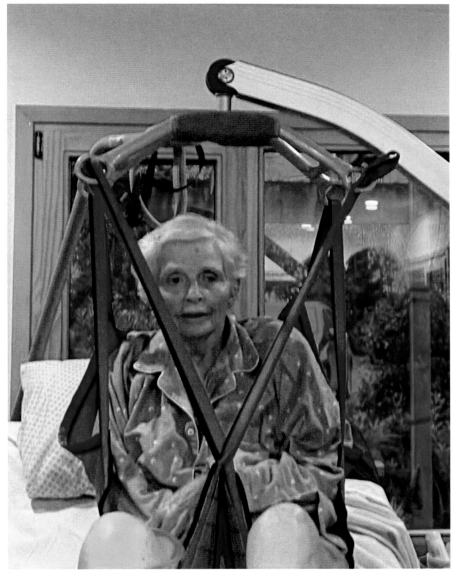

Some anxious moments facial expression

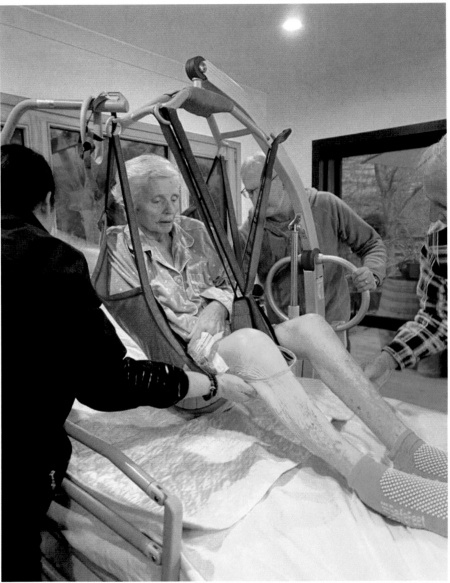

Hoisting is always a two-person activity to ensure safe transfer for Rina.

Safe and secure in lazy boy for a few hours. 30th June 2021

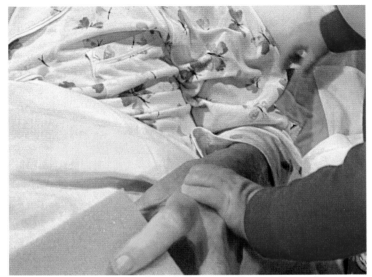

*"I have got you Oumie" , says Great Grandson
Preston Gray Chellew, 2nd July 2021*

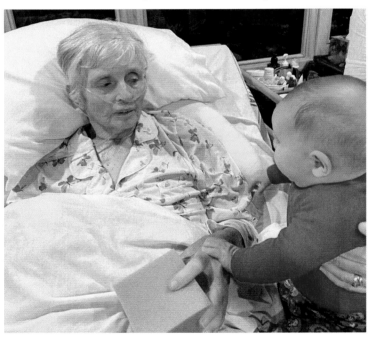

Rina's story

Three of four generations of Geldenhuys family. Great grandmother , grandmother, and grandson.

Great Grandpa Prop and Preston Gray Chellew

Courtney Chellew (nee Jelley) Rina's granddaughter and Preston Gray, great grandchild. Rina now off the syringe driver and onto oral medication. Yet another positive step in journey away from palliative care towards rehabilitation. 2nd July 2021

Great Grand Uncle "OuBeeb" videoed in from his hospital bed in South Africa to support Rina. 4 July 2021. He died the next day.

Great grandma and great grandson Preston Gray Chellew. 3rd July 2021

Great grandparents "pleased as punch"

Son Pey Geldenhuys and granddaughters Lucy and Mia visiting for weekend. 4ᵗʰ July 2021

Preston Gray Chellew meets his uncle, Pey Geldenhuys

Sharing the childcare responsibilities and lots of love.

Preston Gray Chellew looks quite contented

Oumie seems to "nose" what she's doing. Kiss for Preston Gray.

Another milestone. Managing her own cup of rooibos tea. 6th July 2021

Preston Gray Chellew will read this book long after Oumie has
passed away. It will show him what she looked like when he was
way too young to understand the gravity of the occasion. Also –
with the country being at Stage 4 lockdown, his move from
Kakanui to Oamaru to their new home was also put on hold.

First day in motorised wheelchair. 5th July 2021. Rina managed the controls as she has always done.

"Ouma and Oupa sit op die stoep"

A beautiful winters day at Wobble Inn. This time in her manual wheelchair that remains with her since her early stroke days in South Africa.

Rina's story

Watching the wildlife. Guinea fowl and chickens for company.

Enjoying the outdoor trips to catch some rays

The face speaks a thousand words

*15th July 2021. Rina joins us at the dinner table for the first time.
Progress occurs each day and each week.*

Rina's story

A smile can say so much more than all the missing words!

Loving relationship between carer Pam and client Rina. Grateful for genuine amazing care and small gifts. Day 48.

More diversional therapy. Sorting her own pills into a daily medication pack making for easier management and prevent us making mistakes.

Rina's story

Sorting pills into the 'pill-boxes'

Bring on those warm spring days

Prop gone to church First puzzle has started.15th August,202. Love hearing her say" daar is sy" when she finds the interlocking piece. Rina had shown no real interest when offered to her early on in her journey and Prop had finished it himself. Great that Rina challenged to achieve this task.

Graduated to more complex and larger puzzle as part of diversional therapy. 20th August 2021

20th August 2021.

Very proud grandparent Grahame Jelley

The Timeline of Journey

On Monday 24th May Dr Nigel Rajavetnam said that he wanted to meet with Renene and I – after Michelle the physiotherapist was finished with the morning's exercises. We met in the meeting room the next day at 10:45, with my son Pey joining us via smartphone.

Day 1

Rina had a CT scan and her blood tests showed low potassium – reflected in Rina not feeling so good. Her doctor dropped the bombshell that Dr Cameron and Palliative nurse Novelle Farrell will arrange where Rina 'wishes to spend her remaining days – not weeks nor months – before dying.

Options were basically the local Hospice or Beulah home. Rina opted for Kerikeri! Her wishes were conveyed to the Palliative care folk and the head sister worked on several options. We chose the middle road – for a private ambulance trip from the hospital to Wobble-Inn. Grahame Jelley set about arranging a hospital bed, lazy boy chair and a commode for Rina. These took a few days to organise.

The ambulance duly arrived on Friday 28th May – day 4 and uplifted Rina and I from Waikato Hospital.

Hospice nurses Pip and Pam Claire tended to Rina's medication drugs and were later assisted by carer, Kelly Brown who washes and tends to Rina's wellbeing.

Kelly Brown has a very interesting whakapapa – something like 29 family generations, back to her "Tipuna" Rahiri and Ngapuhi Ki Whangaroa iwi. She has two daughters, named Georgia Heni (Janet) Young and Hazel Tui Young, fathered by her partner Daniel Robert Young.

Kelly's parents were Peter Wiremu (Bill) Brown and her mother was Janet Mitchell. She has two sisters – the elder named Ngaire Ann and the second, younger, named Sandra. Kelly's schooling was at an Upper Hut kindergarten then Oxford Crescent School followed by Saint Joseph then Upper Hut College and then Polytech Wellington. She joined Land and Surveying for 16 years and studied Electrical Engineering for two years correspondence course at the University of Queensland. She also has Level Two Support Worker qualification.

Kelly Brown with her two daughters, Georgia and Hazel

Kelly Brown has been most helpful, especially prepared to come tend to Rina during the Stage 4 Lockdown.

Day 10

Thursday, 3rd June 2021. Rina had her hair washed, with Pam helping Renene at the kitchen sink. That evening Pastor Te Hurianga and his wife Rachel gave Rina a surprised visit and prayed for Rina from Ecclesiastes 3 verses 1 to 9 in Maori. There is a RIGHT time for everything – Amen!

The next day Dr Nigel Cain visited Rina on a 'house call' at 6:30 pm when it was pitch black outside. He carried out several test including blood pressure, temperature and listened with his tether scope while Rina breathed deeply. He recommended she go to Kawakawa hospital for blood transfusion and made the necessary ambulance arrangements.

Day 25

Friday, 18th June 2021. A busy day for Rina with next door Lauren visiting plus two Hospice nurses doing meds for Rina and Mary Bowe the occupational therapist carrying out a survey and questionnaire assessment. Sandra from Hospice visited to review medication.

I attended the Kupe Church service held in the Kerikeri Baptist Church.

Monday, 05th July 2021

My brother, Jannie, died after suffering his third heart attack. He had been released from Johannesburg Central hospital the day before. He had been admitted as a Covid patient and had a reasonable recovery albeit needing oxygen to help his breathing. He died when Rina was on Day 42 of Palliative care.

My father's book "The World War II Dairies of ACFP Geldenhuys" was made 'free special offer' with Amazon Kindle.

Watching a movie on Renene's computer – the day Jannie Geldenhuys died in Johannesburg.

Great – Grandmother Rina and great-grandson Preston Gray Chellew

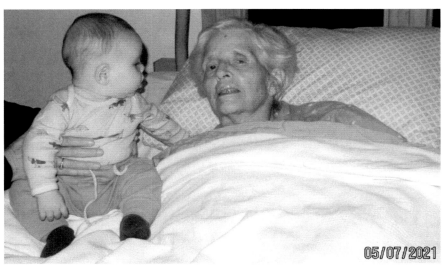

Preston Gray Chellew with Oumie Rina – July 2021

Courtney, Renene, Rina, Grahame, Pey, Lucy and Mia – On day 41

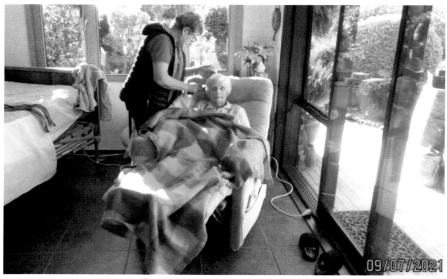

Day 46 – steady progress

Rina's story

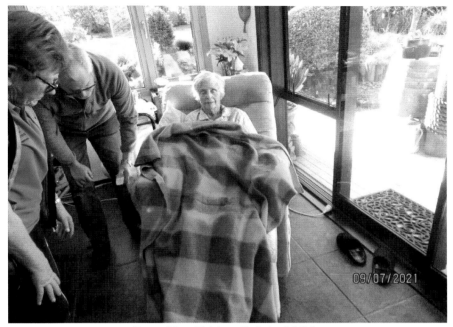

Day 46 – Friday 9 July 2021

Day 50

Tuesday, 13ᵗʰ July 2021.

Dr Nigel Cane carried out a 'house visit' and didseveral medical examinations like taking blood pressure, temperature and examined her urine. He recommended a transfer to Bay of Islands hospital for blood transfusion.

Ann Pidgeon, a clinical nurse Specialist in Gerontology visited Rina. She works for the Northland District Health Board. She visited on Day 64 – Tuesday 27ᵗʰ July 2021.

Time continues to fly buy and we are blown away with the progress Rina has made.

Rina watching streaming channels on computer

The Caravan

Afternoon on the deck of caravan 19th August 2021. Prop made Rina coffee

Rina's first trip to the Campervan

Jack and Jill chair an heirloom from Bill and Mar Jel who had this special seat in Ohope

One of my favourite pictures of a miraculous recovery, thanks for the prayers worldwide and that the timing is all wrong (Waikato staff will be 'most surprised' to see how far Rina has come.

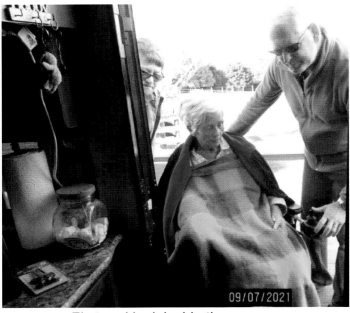

First real look inside the caravan.

Prop explaining to Rina the various aspects of the interior of the caravan.

Rina's story

Enjoying the sunshine – Wobble-Inn'

Prop and Rina relaxing on our deck. We are looking forward to her spending her first night in our new home at Wobble-Inn

Outlook onto the paddocks from caravan deck. Admiring god's rainbow blessing

Dr Grahame Jelley guiding Rina down the ramp

Return journey

Return trip, with Graham a beautiful rainbow complimenting this photo

Grahame Jelley taking over the 'driving' to lineup the ramp onto the deck.

Lining up to go back on deck

Rina's story

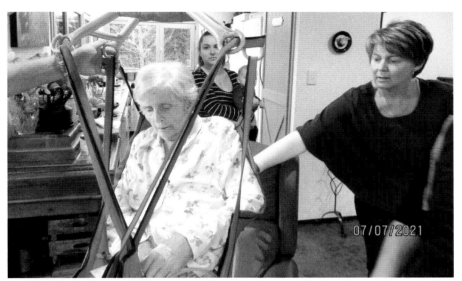

The 'hoist' to get Rina out of her bed – and into a Lazy boy chai

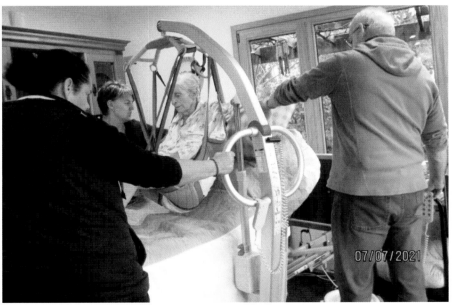

Hoisting Rina back to bed

Grahame taking a selfie of his grandson trying a backstroke while taking his bath

A rather 'cold' Rina – even though her head is well covered

Enjoying the 'outing' with Jade occasional carer in attendance

Duplicated picture – can't find the other (got mixed with my missing marbles!?)

Survival

Physiotherapist Bekki Mills visit to Rina

Bekki attends from the Bay of Islands hospital, Kawakawa and was born in the UK. She visited NZ several years ago and liked the place so much that she made it her new home.

Her first visit to Rina was on Day 70 2nd August but her follow up on about the 23rd – three weeks later, was cancelled due to the lockdown restrictions.

Day 75

Saturday, 7th August 2021. Grahame coughing badly and waited for Renene to return home.

He was admitted to hospital for observation (and missed Renene's birthday).

Flowers arrived!

Celebrating POETs on Renene's birthday with Whakatane visitors Klaus and Minette Kuhn. Minette keeping the dogs occupied.

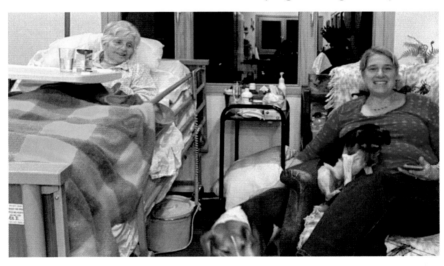

Pey arrived ten day later to take over from the Jellies who had planned an Anniversary celebration with their daughter Courtney and Lewis Chellew in Kakanui, South Island. But one Covid case was identified in Auckland which meant the Prime Minister announcing at 6:10pm that Lockdown country wide being imposed at midnight. Sob!

Survival

Grahame Jelley cancelled his flight bookings and Pey made plans to return to Auckland.

Worked on Preston Gray's fairy tale books – whole day! Also, an Alphabet book.

Monday 23 August – Haircut and Hairdo Day. Rina is losing her hair and will be bald very shortly!

Enjoying the sunshine on the deck – day 89 - Selfie

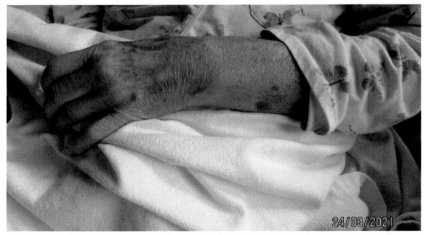

Four bruises – don't know when nor how they occurred.

Rain, rain, go away – come again, another day.

Note the wet deck outside – plenty rain during August 2021.

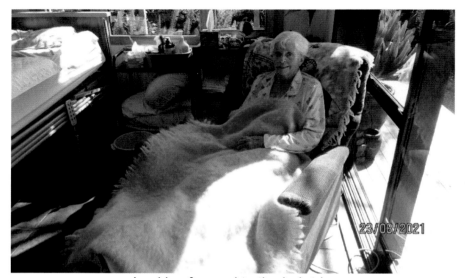

Looking forward to the hair trim

Here today, Hair gone tomorrow

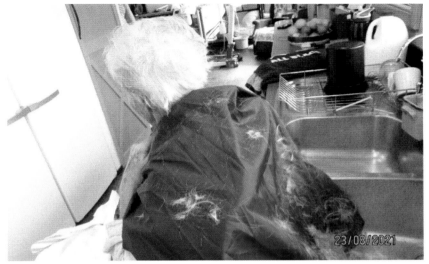

Hair cut equals hairdo!

All smiles with the delivery of a brand-new TV for Rina – so that Prop can get back to the Campervan. Looking cheerfully despite picking up a UTI! Rina is blind in her left eye (from the stroke she had about 30 years earlier)

Survival

A new TV was delivered and Grahame soon had it connected, Renene re-arranged the bed and Lazy boy chair.

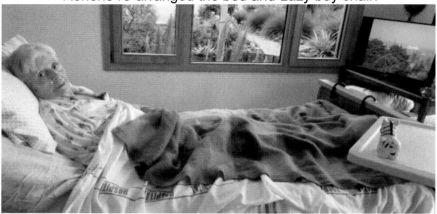

Rina watching the screensaver on TV

Mia Geldenhuys had a fall and fractured her left foot. It was put in a plaster cast

A smart phone hot spot installed so good computer connection in caravan now – Yippee!!

Day 95 (Count down!)

Friday, 27th August 2021

Counting down the last 5 days to the book launch AND keeping track of the days that the good Lord has blessed us as a family.

Rina is eating well (solid foods). She is having 'normal' bowel movements, gaining weight and macking massive mobility movements. There is much hope for the future!

All praise to God, Jesus, and the Holy Spirit.

Rina's story

Rina doing the NZ Picture puzzle

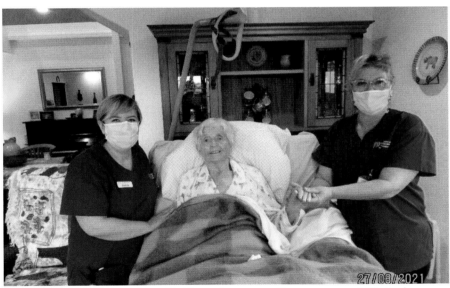

Northern District Health Board nurses Bronwyn and Victoria changed Rina's catheter second change since arrival.

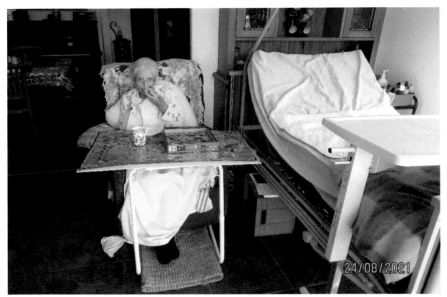

Puzzle time

Monday, 30th August – Rina showing Kelly the drawing.

Rina's story

Saturday 28th August 2021

Count down started – 4 days to book launch.

Sunday 29th August 2021

Day 97 started with a 'Kings Breakfast' of bacon and eggs, flapjacks, fried onions, and tomatoes, "mealie pap" and of course – my Queen – Rina joining us at the table.

She even managed to move from her wheelchair to the lazy-boy – without the hoist! That achievement smile is well worth capturing on camera but Sob – forgot to take the picture.

Rina in Pink

My Queen getting stuck in

The Kings Breakfast

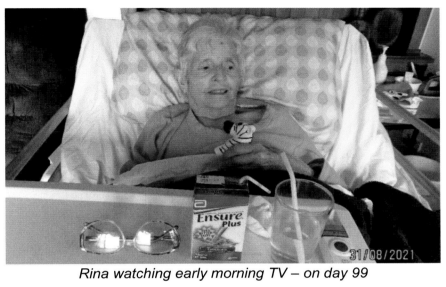

Rina watching early morning TV – on day 99

Starting another puzzle

Rina and Prop – day 99.

Kelly Brown going over her Whakapapa

Day 100 - 1ˢᵗ September 2021

100 days since Dr Nigel Rajaretnam recommended Palliative Care for Rina and that arrangements needed to be made to comply with what the family want done.

Pey contacted Rina's brothers and sisters and the Geldenhuys relatives as well.

The 'count down' picture – from 1 to 100 days

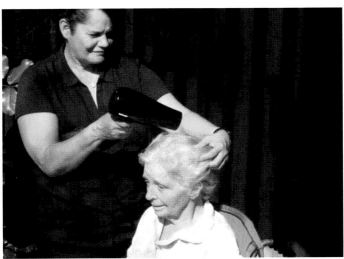

Kelly blow-drying Rina's hair

Rina doing what she does best – colouring in

Kelly Brown brought two 1000-piece puzzels for Rina to tackle.

Rina's story

Prayer warriors (continued from page 15): -

Liz Barrington-Smith: - Each day is a gift + a heart emoji.
Kevin Michael Leonard Barron: + a prayer emoji . Mary Berkhout;
of course, you may publish + a thumbs up emoji. Peter Besant:
Wishing you and Rina all the best. Regards from Pete Besant in
Crawley UK . Truida Bester - Prayers for Rina, God Bless.
Adele and Johan Bezuidenhout. Gerta Bezuidenhout.
Adele Bezuidenhout: Such happy news, hope Rina makes a full
recovery very soon, sending (hugs). Linda Jill Bleeker: -
Thinking of you both - special people 2 heart emoji. Lesley-
Ann Boshoff
Love story and stories of courage and bravery on the part of both of
you. You are so blessed to have each other. Big hugs to you both
and all the people providing family support. Gill Boswell: -
Special love to you and Rina, Prop + 2 heart emoji. Jan
Botha: - Praying for Rina to recover. Debra and Johan
Bouwer Alison Brooker. June Brundle: - Prayers for you both.
Walter and Verna Bruton: - Always in our thoughts and prayers + 2
prayer and three red heart emojis. James Buckley: - Wishing her a
full recovery + 3 prayer emoji. Paul Burmeister + ePub book.
Denise Cain. Sam Cart. Barbara Cameron -- Of course.
you in our prayers always. Audrey Anne Chandler: - Love you Rina
special girl and Prop, you are the most supportive husband ever! A
wonderful union of love and devotion + a red heart and three emoji.
. Dorothy Brown-Arnett: - God willing, Prop. Yes, of course you
can. Thanks for asking. This was a phrase my Gran used a lot and
seems more and more appropriate to life as I get older. Christopher
Ian Clark: - Praying for both of you stay strong and safe in our
current troubled times best wishes for GOD'S HEALING HANDS TO
BE LAID ON RINA + four prayer emoji. Paul Cook: - My thoughts
are with you both. Anne Cooke-Shaw: - Thinking of you, Rina and
you families with love, thoughts, and prayers. Denise Cain: -
Keep positive. Get as many laughs as you can. You can do this.
Hugs. Gavin Carpenter. Diana Clare: - 2 prayer hand either
side of a yellow heart emoji. Mark Cockburn: - Prayer hand.
May Lorraine Craddock: - Wish Rina well. Our prayers are with you.

2 Prayer hand emoji.   John Connolly "Punchy".   May Lorraine Craddock; Martha Magdalene Crossley. Jenny and Ian Cruickshank: - Well done all of you. Love and God bless you all - the Cruicks. No problem, Prop (to print). Malcolm Dale (since deceased); Roy Darkin: - God bless both of you. Thanks Roy - much has happened since I ordered your book - - - now to find it again to send to you (We relocated to Kerikeri, and all my books need a new home to be found) + a heart emoji.   Davies : + a prayer emoji.   Alan D'Agviar.   Yvonne de Kock. Salome de Oliveira.   Estie Nel de Jager.   Antoinette Dick.   Ann Donnelly: - Prayers for Rina... a full recovery   .   John Dovey. Geoff Dunne: - Sorry to hear that boet. Hope she goes well + emogi. Print with pleasure Prop + a prayer emoji.   Veronica Murdoch Eaton.   Bruce Edward.   Elizabeth Eggar. Coralie Eichler: - We will have to call you the comeback kid. Looking forward to your complete recovery and healing. God is a miracle man. Yes, you can [Publish].   Della Ferreira: - May God bless and protect you both – 2 double red heart emoji. Of course, you may publish. Hope and trust you are both doing well - 2 double red heart emoji.   Jean Fletcher.   Carole Fourie.   Marieke Fourie.   Paul Friedrich.   Bronwyn Grey Fulton. Carolyn Galbraith: I miss seeing you on Sundays Rina, many spiritual blessings to you dear heart. Love from Carolyn Galbraith. Hi Carolyn - Rina is now on day 64, She has been taken off the Palliative Care list and will see a therapist later today (losing the use of her remaining limb - her left hand has developed 'twitching' - like Parkinson's) - but all glory to GOD for sparing her SO LONG! I am now doing a book on her experience and would love to add your comments . Jonathan Gale.   Paul and Karen Geldenhuys. Pey, Matthew, Lucy, and Mia Geldenhuys.   Helen Wightman Gent.   Brent Gerhardt.   Elaine Child.. Nico Germishuizen: - Keep the faith Prop. Keeping it - God is good, all the time. Charles Gibbon.   John Gifford: - Thinking and our prayers for your wife and you and your family in this time be strong and keep your eyes and faith on our Saviour Jesus Christ our king God bless.   June Gohery. Jillian Grimbeek: - Must be a strong lady. Best

wishes to you all xxx.   Tish Gooding. Brian   Goodwin: - Our thoughts are with you. our mighty God is with you and family may His strength sustain you. Kathy Graydon: - Sending you both strength & prayers + a smiley face and a prayer emoji.   Jean Greene.   Sylvia Geldenhuys: - Rina is safe in God's caring hands. Sending lots of love to both. Stay safe - 2 double red heart emoji.   Kathy Graydon: - Bless you both + 2 imogi. Katerwa Halaris, Elmeri Wheeler Harley.   Bill Harley.   Arthur   Murray Harmsworth + 3 emoji.   Gillian Hill.   Rhoda   Holland: +   7 prayer emojis.   Ingrid and Steve Howard.   Glen   Seymour Hall.   Elmerie Wheeler Harley: - In our thoughts & prayers constantly.

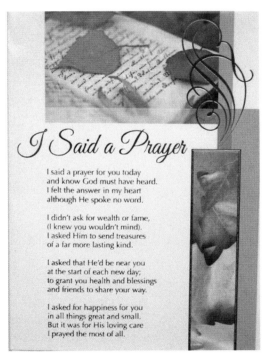

Hilary Hartley. Maureen McElroy Hayes.   Vincent   Heaney: - Thoughts and prayers are with you - + prayer hands emogi. No problem at all, to print.   Frances Hill: - Thoughts with you both.Rhoda Holland: - Prayers with you both + 5 prayer hands and 3 smiley faces - yes anytime. I honestly do pray dear friend.　　Kim Hooton-Fox Debbie Huxham.　　Mem Hughes-Seaman: - Rooting for your recovery. Wendy Ireland. Peta Jacobs. Doug Jardine: - Prayer hand emoji. Renene and Grahame Jelley. Dave　Jenkins.　Cliff　and　Patricia Kershaw: - That's amazing.　Ken and Dawn Kershaw.　　Elsa Kleinhans.　　Marieta Kluckow.　　Jacqui Kirrane.　　Elaine Knott: - In our prayers Prop. + 2 prayer hands. Leon Kok: - Wishing her all of the best + emoji. Joy Lambie.　Linda Law.　　Carmen Ledger. Brian Lennon-Smith.　Beverley Levi: - Amazing what prayer can do. Stay strong dear lady. It's working!!! Kelly Levi: - God always there for us, He's take care for those who trust him, Rina she's one of those, God show his wonderful love through her, our prayers continue lift her to our heavenly father and Jesus our Lord.　Joe Martins: - You and your family are in my thoughts Prop. Small steps, one day at a time.

Mike Layard;- Certainly Brother!　Joy Lambie: - God bless her xx absolutely　[to publish].- If you stop 'the dash' will become meaningless God bless Rina .... strength to you and your family.
　　Brian Lennon-Smith: - she will see you out Prop, ...in many years' time. Janet Marchussen: - Going well ! Good for you Rina x I don't mind at all Prop.　Peter MacDonald: - Our thoughts and prayers for you both.　Gordon　Mckeith:　-　Thoughts　and Prayers + a two-prayer emoji.　Jacqui Kirrane: - My thoughts and prayers are with you both, Prop - double red heart emoji.

170

Rina's story

Tracey O'Connor: - She is feeling the love around her, I am sure. Thinking of you. Des Thea Coetzer: - Praying for Rina + a prayer emoji. Ray Haakonsen: - In His time.....prayers with you Boss Prop . Ccertainly + a two-prayer emoji. Glenn Seymour Hall: - A fighter may she rest a while longer with you. Of course, you can (print). Love prayers and best wishes to you and the family.
Gillian Hill. Mike Jones: + three prayer emoji. Francois Joubert: - You and Rina are in our thoughts and prayers.100%. Joy Lambie: - it's all about THE DASH ... you cannot stop. Mike Layard: - Love you, Rina ! May God give you strength, courage to fully recover. Linda Law. Brian Lennon-Smith; Beverley Levi; Penduka Luis: - Prays with you both + a prayer emoji. Frans and Keinding Malan (brother); Phil and Elcora Malan (brother); Anaela Mason (ex Esterhuizen). . Clive Mayo. Dee and Stu McColl. John Bryan McDonell. Ian McFarlane. Ken McKittrick: - My thoughts are with you Prop + a prayer emoji. Prop Geldenhuys: - I was about to stop counting the days BUT a kindly lady (Pam - you know who I am speaking of?) challenged me to keep the count going to reach 100!!?? Maybe I should, ek se??
Lorraine Mitchell. John Mussell. Robin Napier. Martin Nel. Willem Andries Stephanus Nel. Ana Guerreiro Neto: - Praying for you all + a prayer emoji. Ana Guerreiro Neto: - yes, you can – one heart emoji. Beverley Nelson. Debbie Nelson: - My love to you & your dear wife - double red heart emoji. Peter Nisbet; David Noakes; Anne Olivier: - Praise God for His Mercy & Love!
Kathleen Antlett Paintin: - Rina is built of sturdy stuff, there have been many battles over the years for us Rhodesians. Wishing her strength in her current battle. Wishing you strength too Prop, and your family who are supporting you. Ross Palmer. Mike Peake: - Our love and prayers are with you Rina and Prop.
Pam Perry: - Bless you. Judith Petrou: - I hold you both in my prayers. Kevin Pott. Marcus Proome: -Praying for you all.
Gordon Radloff: - two smiley faces and 4 prayer hands.
Barry Ashley Roberts. Phil Runciman: - Well Prop, I believe in miracles... this is one of the more dramatic... precious time together!
Farmboy Sambane; - and several Facebook mates . Mags

Sayers.　　Daphne Seiler: - God Bless her in her struggle.
Alex, Maureen and Colleen Scott. Hazel　Sittig:　+　a　two-prayer
emoji.　　Hugh and Jayne Slatter.　　Tony and Shirlee Smit.
　　Sandi Spence: - Both of you are in our prayers Prop.
Irene Steyn: - Sending much love and blessings to you all Prop +
emogis.　　Louis Stopforth: - God bless Prop and Rina, there has
been much improvement, so great to see and in the best hands of
care, wish the best for all of you. Anne-Marie　Stannard-Scott:　-
Sending my thoughts and prayers and YES God is certainly a
Miracle worker, in many, many ways + 3 emogi. I love prayers and
more so when our prayers are answered. Thinking of you both at
this time Prop. Take good care + 2 emogi.　　Jacqui Smith: -
Huge hugs and prayers - 4 double red heart emoji and 6 prayer
hands.　　Beaver Shaw: - Best wishes and God bless you and
Rina. Beaver Shaw: - Of course you may. Edward Shepherd: -
Prayers.　　Daderian Stewart: - My thoughts and prayers are with
you both at this time – smiley face emoji. Elsie　Stoltz; Blessings,
Prop and Rina, thinking of you. You certainly may publish, Prop, it
will be an honor, Praying for Rina to soon be well and enough
strength to be up and about, also for you to be strong in prayer and
faith, best regards my friend, you may publish any message you
would like to. Lesley Strydom.　　Maureen Geldenhuys Trichardt:
- I'm very bad useful for you my Sus Marita Brodie (Geldenhuys)
what a complete pedigree it's of that Geldenhuys' died last night
Greetings.　　Barry Johnstone-Robertson: - Our love and prayers for
you both mate – one heart and a prayer emogi.　　Paul Mroz: - With
both of you in spirit Prop.　　Rachel and　Ps Te Hurihanga Rihari.
　　Shereen Thompson: - Amazing.: - So sorry to hear this. It's
tough on the sufferer and the ones who love them. Wonderful to
hear she is a fighting gal and we pray for all Cancer sufferers. You
take care as well. No problem at all. Shared with Your friends and
Marita's friends. I really miss Marita Brodie - she died 8 years ago
in 2013.　　.　　; Bruce Upton: - Still in My Thoughts and
Prayers.　　Aletta van Aardt (Rina's eldest sister),　　Adrianna
van Biljon.　Chantal van der Linden;　　Andre van der Merwe – 2
prayer and a rose emoji.　　Izak van der Merwe: - In our prayers

Rina's story

Prop – thumbs up emoji.   Angie van Nuil: - Sending good strong vibes. Charlie van Schalkwyk.   Jimmy Van Vuuren: - Prop I think you have been hacked + three prayer and a red heart emoji. I have no problem Prop. God bless you both. Don't worry?   Magda Ferreira van Zyl: - Prop, that is amazing + heart emogi. Dit moet al die gebede wees wat vir haar opgaan en natuurlike ook die wonderlike sorg wat sy kry + exclamation emogi - Met plesier + heart emogi.   Mario Venutti: - In our thoughts Prop.   Sue Walsh: - This is the time to be able to share the stories and love that you all have in your supportive family + flower emoji. Prop Geldenhuys; - I am compiling it - taken a slight back seat to re-write and compile it. I will appreciate it if I may include your comments? May I publish your name (Facebook)? Sue Walsh said "Course you can. I give you the rights to all of my com. Keep up with the count. Give Rina a hug from the Coast." .   .   Carole Ward. Quinn Ward: - She's a fighter!!!   Peter Watson: My thoughts are with you and Rina. Chunky George Webster: - In our thoughts and prayers Prop and Rina xx. George and Tarns xx,   Jenny Whelehan.   Rosemary Whittle: - Yes...hearts all out to both of you!   Terry Winsor.   Andrew Williams: - That's so great to see, Prop. May she remain well and able for many years still to come. Rob Williams.   Ken Wilson: - We will pray for full healing. God Bless. Gayle Windrim: - My thoughts and prayers are with you both + 2 emogi. Terry Winsor.   Patricia Wright: - Best wishes and prayers for you both Prop + 10 emoji. Of course, xx [you may publish]. Prop Geldenhuys: - Now day 63 + 426 likes AND 227 comments. WOW!! Just + heart emogi - them ALL!!

Laurence Wentzel sent a daily – sometimes twice daily, scripture passages, like - Jesus Christ – {Edited. Reviewed} Unity!!!... Be one!!!... "I am Jesus Christ, the Son of God, who was crucified for the sins of the world, even as many as will believe on my name, that they may become the sons of God, even one in me as I am one in the Father, as the Father is one in me, that we may be one" (D+C 35 : 2).

"And now I am no more in the world, but these are in the world, and I come to thee. Holy Father, keep through thine own name those whom thou hast given me, that they may be one, as we are. Neither pray I for these alone, but for them also which shall believe on me through their word ; That they all may be one ; as thou, Father, art in me, and I in thee, that they also may be one in us : that the world may believe that thou hast sent me. And the glory which thou gavest me I have given them; that they may be one, even as we are one : I in them, and thou in me, that they may be made perfect in one ; and that the world may know that thou hast sent me, and hast loved them, as thou hast loved me" (N.T. John 17 : 11, 21-23).

The imagery of the "seven golden candlesticks" (N.T. Rev. 1 : 12, 20) recalls the seven-branched menorah found in the Jerusalem temple. These candlesticks represented the seven churches.

The Saviour said that His disciples "are the light of the world" and should not "put {their light} under a bushel, but on a candlestick" (N.T. Matt. 5 : 14–15). The Greek word translated as "candlestick" here is the same word translated from "menorah" in the Greek Old Testament {Septuagint}.

In John's vision, he saw Jesus Christ "in the midst of the seven candlesticks," showing symbolically that He was with or among the seven ancient churches (N.T. Rev. 1 : 13). During His mortal ministry, Jesus promised, "Where two or three are gathered together in my name, there am I in the midst of them" (N.T. Matt. 18 : 20). The assurance that Jesus Christ is with His Saints and watches over them is also found in modern scripture "Verily, verily, I say unto you that mine eyes are upon you. I am in your midst and ye cannot see me" (D+C 38 : 7).

The importance of John referring to Candlesticks is that they carry light ; they do not create it. Their function is to make it available, not to bring it into being. So, by using seven candlesticks to portray the seven churches to whom John is now to give counsel, the Lord is showing that His congregations on earth are to carry His light to the world. Christ is the Light of the world. (N.T. John 8 : 12). "Hold up your light that it may shine unto the world. Behold I am the light which ye shall hold up. That which ye have seen me do" (B.O.M. 3 Nephi 18 :

24 Edited ; N.T. Matt. 5 : 14–16.). The greater view of the seven churches is that this number seven in representative of the completeness and unity of His True Church upon the earth in these latter days. Each individual disciple needs to strive for unity with Jesus Christ and with the collective Church to exemplify that oneness that exists between Christ and His Church, for as a collective, the Church of Christ holds up the Light of Christ.

When the disciples gather together and are in the process individually and collectively of obtaining the character and nature of Jesus Christ, who said, "If a man love me, he will keep my words : and my Father will love him, and we will come unto him, and make our abode with him" (N.T. John 14 : 23).

This Presence of the divine is not that which is experienced by individual believers when both the Father and the Son make their abode with them but rather this is when disciples gather together seeking the "face" of Jesus Christ and God our Father for vital revelation as in the case of the reception of the confirmation of Declaration 2, when the Lord opened the door for all worthy men irrespective of race to receive the priesthood in 1978, thus showing the importance of following the Redeemers example of unity among the God Head in order to receive revelation. This gives disciples a preview of what they can expect in the Millennium when Jesus Christ reigns upon the earth, and furthermore when all exalted disciples will dwell in both the Presence of the Elohim and Jesus Christ in the Celestial Kingdom.

"Where there is Light, there is Love".

"Where there is no Light, there is no Love". Postings.

My sincere apologies if you can't find your name in the index (look for it with your facebook – first name). If you still can't find it then please email Prop at prop@peysoft.co.za and I will make an update in the print edition – when next I get to search myself.

Index

Rina's story

Rina's story

179

Survival

Email the author: prop@peysoft.co.za

ISBN: 9798479869228

Links: -

This book (ePub) – https://www.amazon.com/dp/B09F6115VC

B&W version –

Colour edition – 9798479869228

Other Serial books –

   Wonky Honkey - https://www.amazon.com/dp/B08XWYWXXG

   Air Force -https://www.amazon.com/dp/1728831334

   Nickel Cross – https://www.amazon.com/dp/1539980405

   Wacky Quack - https://www.amazon.com/dp/B09BCCDKHT

New Zealand –

A Grave New Zealand Story –
https://www.amazon.com/dp/B087637FCV

Thank you for your support and especially your prayers for Rina.

(Do click on 'Look Inside' to see much more content. Also, please click on the 'authors name' to see a listing of more books).

Made in United States
Orlando, FL
17 June 2022